How to Write a Nonfiction Book and Publish It on Amazon

A Complete Step-By-Step Beginner's Guide to Writing and Publishing Your First Book—at Zero Cost

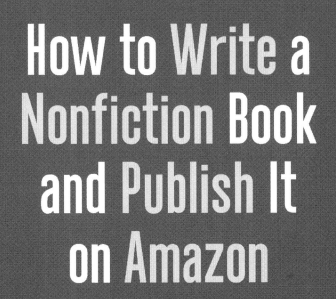

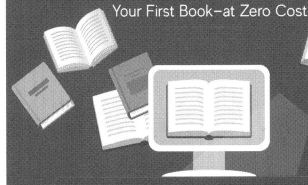

Jerry Minchey

Disclaimer

The information in this book is based on the author's knowledge, experience, and opinions. The methods described in this book are not intended to be a definitive set of instructions. You may discover other methods to accomplish the same end result. Your results may differ.

There are no representations or warranties, express or implied, about the completeness, accuracy, or reliability of this book's information, products, services, or related materials. The information is provided "as is" to be used at your own risk.

This book is not intended to give legal, financial, or medical advice. It is sold with the understanding that the author is not engaged in rendering legal, accounting, medical, or other professional services or advice. If legal, financial, or medical advice or other expert assistance is required, the services of a competent professional should be sought to ensure you fully understand your obligations and risks.

Contents

Chapter 1

Introduction

"There are three rules for writing the novel. Unfortunately, no one knows what they are."

~ W. Somerset Maugham

That's why I don't write novels. I write only nonfiction books.

Note: The original version of this book was published in 2022. I updated the book in 2024. This new version contains the latest up-to-date information—**including Amazon's recent rules changes**. There were some major changes in Chapter 12 about selecting categories, and changes in several other chapters. I also corrected a few typos.

There are 1,080 authors on Amazon who make over $50,000 a year from their book sales, and I'm one of those. My sales went down during the pandemic, but they're coming back up. I didn't do it with one book. I've published over 20 books on Amazon.

I assume you want to write a book to make money. If you want to write your memoirs for your grandkids to read, this is probably not the right book for you to be reading. This book aims to show you how to write your first book, publish it on Amazon, and make money with it.

Warren Buffett said it best: *"If you don't find a way to make money while you sleep, you'll work until you die."*

Having a book published and listed on Amazon is one of the best ways I know to make money while you sleep.

In addition to making money with your book, writing a book will also help establish you as an authority in your field.

If you own a business, whether a sticks-and-bricks or an online business, writing a book will help establish you as an industry leader and an authority in your field.

When you're meeting movers and shakers in your field, you won't be handing them a business card they'll soon lose or throw away. You can give them a copy of your book. That will establish you as an expert in your field.

Adding the word "Author" or "Author of the best-selling book xyz" to your resume or bio will help move you to the top of the heap.

Picture yourself as a writer

Picture yourself sitting in a coffee shop writing your book. Can you see yourself in the picture on the next page?

When you're a writer, you can work anywhere.

When you can make money writing books, you'll have a location-independent source of income, and you can travel and work anywhere in the world and write on your own schedule.

To make this happen, you have to get started and write your first book. You're well on your way because you're reading this book to learn how to write and publish your first book on Amazon. Keep reading and following the steps outlined herein, and you'll have your first book published before you know it.

Writer's Digest magazine recently reported that 81% of Americans think they should write a book, but only 2% have completed a manuscript.

When you write and publish your book, you'll have accomplished something that most people only dream about.

This book is not about theory. The techniques I describe in this book are all tried and proven. I've written over 20 books using these techniques, and I know they work. Many of the books I've written have become bestsellers in their categories.

Here are some vital steps in the book-writing process that many self-publishers miss

Your book should be about one very narrow topic. It shouldn't be general information or try to cover a broad market niche.

For example, this book is not about how to write or even how to write a book. It's about how to write a nonfiction book.

I could have included a chapter about how to write a novel and tried to appeal to a broader audience by having a title saying something about how to write a book. In my opinion, that would have hurt my sales big time. And besides, I don't know anything about writing a novel. I've never done it.

Your main goal should be to provide value to the reader. Don't try to tell the reader everything you know about a topic. Your purpose should not be just to inform but to transform the reader. That's what the reader wants when they buy your book.

Readers don't want information. They want a transformation.

Read this statement again. It's important for you to keep this point in mind as you write your book.

The best Internet business in the world

A lot of people dream of having an internet business. I've run different online Internet businesses for over 20 years, and by far, what I consider to be the best Internet business is writing and publishing books on Amazon.

When you list your books for sale on Amazon, you will eliminate most of the problems and expenses of running a business.

You don't have to keep an inventory of the products you're selling; you don't need a merchant account; you don't have to take orders, process orders, calculate the sales taxes you need to collect for each state, and you don't have to bother with returns.

The money shows up in your checking account each month—and it all happens regardless of where in the world you are at any given time. When you sell books on Amazon, you'll have an Internet business, and you don't even need a website. You can spend your time writing more books.

Your goal should be quality—not speed

Don't write a crappy book.

You want to write a quality book. That doesn't mean it should take you forever.

There are books and videos that tell you how to write a book fast or in a weekend. I've never written a book in a weekend, but I have written two books in less than 30 days each. By 30 days, I mean from when I wrote the first word until I had a copy of the book in my hand.

Neither of those two books was a bestseller. I've also worked on a book for over a year, but that wasn't one of my bestsellers, either.

Your goal shouldn't be to write a book in 30 days. Your goal should be to write a bestseller. You can do it with your first book if you follow the advice and steps I describe in this book.

Several of my books have been on Amazon's Bestseller list in their category. I've even had a time when the #1 and

#2 Best-Selling books were my books in one category. Is it a good or bad thing if you can't get your book to move up from #2 to #1 because one of your other books is ranked #1?

Below is a screenshot from Amazon showing two of my books ranking #1 and #2 in the Senior Travel Guides category.

My books ranked #1 and #2 in Amazon's Senior Travel Category.

Speaking of competition, someone gave one of my books a four-star review a few years ago. He commented that he would have given me a five-star review, but no book is perfect—except the Bible. I didn't know I had to compete with the Bible.

Books don't stay ranked #1 forever. That's why it's important to keep writing more books and promoting the ones you have written.

Your first book is the hardest. After you've written one book, writing your second book is much easier. We'll talk about that later.

In this book, I'll show you step-by-step how to write and publish your book for zero cost. I will show you two or more ways to do things for the steps involved.

The first way will be how to do the step yourself for zero cost. If you take the time to follow my directions and learn how to do each step, you can write and publish your book (and have a printed copy in your hands) and not spend a penny.

The additional ways I'll show you is how you can hire an expert for some of the steps and get your book written and published faster (and possibly have a more professional-looking book) by spending a small amount of money.

It's not an either-or process. You can do some of the steps all by yourself and pay for some professional help for others. That's the way I do it. I've published books where I've done every step by myself, designing the cover, doing my own proofreading, etc. Surprisingly, one of the books I published this way was (and still is) one of my bestsellers.

If you follow the steps in this book, you can soon be holding a book you wrote in your hand—and the whole process can be free.

I usually pay someone to design my covers, and I hire a professional proofreader (as well as have several friends proofread my manuscript).

You can write and publish your book, and inside the book, you can dedicate it to your mother. Then, hand her the book. She will be even prouder of you than she already is. That should be enough of a reason to get you started writing your first book.

When writing and publishing your first book, there are advantages to doing every step of the process yourself. Remember that you can go back after the book is published and change anything about the book except the title and subtitle. You can completely change the cover, correct errors, change the text, and change the formatting. Don't worry if your first book is not perfect. "Done trumps everything."

If you have a little money to spend on the project, I suggest hiring a professional proofreader. If you have a little more money to invest in your book project, you should consider hiring someone to design your book cover.

I'll show you how to do all those things yourself in this book. I've published books both ways.

Don't worry if you think you can't write. I can't write either, and plenty of English teachers agree that I can't write. I'm an engineer, and I've never made a grade higher than a C in a college English class, but now I make my living writing books.

There are other benefits to writing and publishing a book

Here are some of the many benefits you'll get in addition to making money:

- When you have written and published a book, you're considered an expert and authority on your topic. In other words, a lot of prestige comes with being an author.

- When you've written a book, it automatically puts you in a higher echelon of people who have accomplished something.

- Most people would love to have written a book (and many secretly desire to write one someday). They'll admire you because you've done what they wish they could do.

Several books listed on Amazon promise to show you how to write and publish a book. The goal of this book is not to be one of the many books on the topic but to be the very best and most complete and comprehensive book on the subject.

The most important thing that sets this book apart from the competition is that I'll show you the techniques I've used to make writing your book easier, faster, and more profitable than you ever thought it could be.

Don't fall for the latest fad

Writing low-content books is a popular fad, but I recommend you stay out of this field. A low-content book is a logbook, journal, diary, etc.; in other words, a book with mostly blank pages for people to write in. Some people have made a lot of money with these books, but now I think the market is saturated. Don't go there. Write a nonfiction book.

A well-researched, well-written, and informative book is what you need to have a successful nonfiction book that will sell well over the long run.

In this book, I will not only show you step-by-step how to write and publish your book on Amazon, but I will also show you the strategies necessary to write and publish a book and make money with it.

To earn enough money on Amazon to make an income you can live on, you may need to publish several books, but maybe not.

Things to keep in mind as you write your book

- Finish your book. Don't keep tweaking it. You

can always go back and make changes after it's published. How much money do you make from a book that's almost ready to be published?

- Set a deadline for how many words a day you're going to write or how many hours you will write. Then, make sure you meet that goal. Don't think you're going to find the time to write. Peter De Vries said, *"I only write when I'm inspired, so I see to it that I'm inspired every morning at nine o'clock."* That's the way I write. When I sit down to write, I usually write until noon, and sometimes I'll write all day. A lot of writers say they write for an hour a day. That doesn't work for me. When I get on a roll, I keep going. My most productive time is first thing in the morning. I like to start writing early and keep going as long as the words flow freely, usually until noon and sometimes longer. Find your rhythm and follow that every day. Instead of writing a set number of words a day, I like to have a goal of writing a chapter a day. Go with whatever works for you.

- **A great Introduction is essential.** Hook the reader with something profound. Make a bold promise of what you'll deliver to the reader—but make sure you deliver on that promise.

- **What would you promise if you had godlike power to grant any benefit you wanted to your**

reader? You don't have that kind of power, but how close can you come? What's the greatest benefit you can promise and then deliver to your reader? That's what you should promise—and then deliver it in your book. Give this concept a lot of thought.

- **As you write the book, sometimes you'll find yourself venturing off in different directions from what you had in mind.** You'll find that you've covered some points in a different chapter or that some points in the *Table of Contents* don't need a separate chapter. Delete that chapter and include the point you wanted to make in another chapter. **Change the *table of contents*—don't change the book.**

- **Have a fantastic and profound ending for your book.** Maybe even have this for every chapter in your book, if possible.

- **Turn off your internal editor while you're writing.** Wait until at least the next day before you try to edit your writing. Ernest Hemingway said, "Write drunk. Edit sober." I think that advice works better for fiction than nonfiction, but you should write with an uninhibited mind, even for nonfiction. Let the words flow, and don't try to critique your work while you're writing.

- **Your fantastic idea will not overcome sloppy writing.**

- **You don't want a self-published book that looks like one.**

- **Good writing is based on strong nouns and verbs, not adjectives. Use adjectives sparingly.**

- **Delete the word "that" in most cases. Use it only when it's absolutely needed for clarity.**

- **The Introduction is the most critical part of your book.** Put a lot of thought into it. Then, reread it and tweak it often. It may be the only chapter the reader reads. If he doesn't like the Introduction, he may just stop reading and leave a bad review. Also, most of the time, people can read the Introduction chapter of your book by clicking on the "Look inside" feature on Amazon before they decide to buy your book. You may not sell many books if you don't have a compelling Introduction.

- **You want the Introduction to instill in the reader that this book is a high-quality book that will deliver on everything promised.** Convince prospective readers that your book will solve their problems and answer their questions.

- **Be sure to read the table of contents of other**

books about your topic to see what points they're covering.

- **Look at the reviews of other books about your topic.** See what the readers liked and didn't like about the other books covering your subject. The three-star reviews have the most information. They usually say, "I liked this about the book, and I didn't like that." This is valuable information. Be sure to read all of the three-star reviews.

- **The title of each chapter needs to make a compelling reason why the reader should read that chapter.**

- **Publishing is the place to be today.** There's no better way to make money today than to write and publish books.

- **At age 24, Stephen King worked as a janitor and lived in a trailer.**

- **Grandma Moses didn't begin her painting career until age 76.**

- **At age 28, J.K. Rowling was a suicidal single parent living on welfare.** Then she wrote Harry Potter.

- **There's a low barrier to entry into the self-publishing industry.** Almost anybody can get a book published and do it for zero investment. To be successful, you must find a way to make your book stand out.

- Your book's purpose is to impact someone's life. Keep this concept in mind as you write.

Make sure your book accomplishes this. You see the world differently. You want your readers to see the world the way you do. That's the whole purpose of your book.

Before you start writing your book, make sure you have **MS Word** or the free, open-source program **Libre Office** on your computer. Use one of these programs to write your manuscript.

More than 600,000 books are published annually in the United States and approximately 2.2 million, or 6,000 a day, worldwide.

Since there are 6,000 new books published every day, the day you publish your book, there'll be 6,001 new books published that day. If you want your book to be noticed, follow the advice in every chapter of this book. Each step is essential—your book cover, description, introduction, etc.

Back up your work every day. Back up your work to an external hard drive or thumb drive, or use another method that works for you. I back my work up in three ways. I have a subscription with Carbonite to back up my whole computer automatically every day. I also back up my work on an external hard drive, and then I attach the file to an email that I send to myself at the end of the day.

It's not a matter of IF your computer is going to crash but when. All computers fail sooner or later. My main computer has a solid-state drive (SSD), and that's more reliable than a conventional hard disk drive (HHD), but I still don't trust it. That's why I back my work up every day.

One final point: If you're unsure what topic to write about, jump ahead and read Chapter 18: *How to Find a Profitable Topic for Your Next Book.*

The main takeaway from this chapter: You can write a quality book that will solve people's problems and transform their lives if you follow the techniques in this book, but you have to stay motivated to make it happen. Writing a book is hard work. That's why most people never do it. They only dream about it.

Chapter 2

Why Do You Want to Write a Book?

"It's none of their business that you have to learn how to write. Let them think you were born that way."

~ Ernest Hemingway

Writing a book takes a lot of your time. You must be committed if you want to write, edit, finish, publish, and market a book. If you don't have a clear, compelling reason why you want to write your book, don't waste your time because your book will likely never be finished.

A lot of people would like to have written a book, but not many want to put in the effort it takes to get a book written and published.

Think long and hard about why you want to write a book. Obviously, you have a good reason, or you wouldn't have bought this book. You've taken the first step. That's more than most people ever do.

Take the time to jot down why you want to write a book and what it is you want to accomplish by writing your first book. Without a clear reason why you want to write your book, it won't happen.

Here are some of the reasons why people want to write a book

- To be recognized as an authority on the topic or in your field. (Publishing a book will do that for you.)

- To be a digital nomad and travel while making money.

- To be a paid speaker at conventions and industry events. (When you write a book on a topic, you're considered to be one of the experts in the field.)

- To bring more customers into your business.

- To create another income stream. (Selling books.)

If you're writing your first book to make money, don't write fiction

Some people make a lot of money writing fiction, but it's not easy, and it's not what you should do for your first book. Here's why.

- There's too much you need to know to write good fiction. You have to know how to do character development, plot development, write dialog, and the list goes on.

- When you write fiction, you eliminate a large percentage of readers. Most people who read fiction don't buy printed books or audiobooks—they buy eBooks.

- You won't get as many sales from people searching for your topic as you do with nonfiction books. With nonfiction books, people find your book because they have a problem and want to know how to solve it. They search for the keywords that describe their problem. This doesn't happen with novels. If you don't have a large following or an email list, you'll have to spend a lot of money on ads to get sales. And when you stop spending money, your sales will likely die. You may have to spend a lot of money as a new, unknown fiction author to get your book noticed. Here's a word of advice. If you're going to write fiction, plan on writing a series of at least three books.

- You have to be promoting a fiction book constantly. A nonfiction book can have a life of its own and continue to bring in sales year after year with no effort on your part. Some of my best-selling books are books I wrote five or six years ago. They continue to bring in money month after month. And I've never spent a dime on advertising.

Don't get me wrong; if you like to write fiction and are good at it, you can make money writing fiction. I have friends who make a lot of money writing fiction. A good fiction book can make ten times more than a nonfiction book, but if you're a beginning author and want to write your first book to make money, my advice is not to write a fiction book.

To succeed and make money as a nonfiction writer, you must provide value to your readers. Your book has to answer the reader's question or solve his problem and do it efficiently. Don't ramble and waste the reader's time. Your job as a nonfiction writer is to help people.

The process of writing a book will force you to be curious. And, no, curiosity didn't kill the cat. It made the cat happier.

Here's how: Studies have shown a link between curiosity and dopamine levels. An increase in curiosity results in higher dopamine levels. WebMD says that dopamine levels play a role in how we feel pleasure.

Conclusion. Work on writing a book, and you'll be happier. And when you start selling your book and making money, you'll be even happier still.

The process of writing a book gives you purpose.

When writing a book you feel passionate about, you have a sense of purpose and empowerment.

Writing a book will give you confidence. The famous author William Price Fox said almost everyone would like to have written a book, but not many people want to write a book.

After you write your book, you'll be in the unique category of people who have written a book.

The main takeaway from this chapter: I'm sure you have your reason why you want to write a book, or you wouldn't have bought this one. Maybe you have several reasons. Make sure you keep these reasons in mind as you write your book. That will keep you motivated and ensure that your book gets written and published.

Chapter 3

How to Select Your Most Profitable Keywords

"Most writers regard the truth as their most valuable possession, and therefore are most economical in its use."

~ Mark Twain

Selecting the right keywords is the most important thing you can do to have a successful book—that's why this is the longest chapter in the book. Before you start writing, put a lot of effort into selecting the best keywords and keyword phrases for your book.

You may want to read over this chapter hurriedly to get an overview of the topic and then come back and reread it in detail when you're ready to start selecting your keywords.

Here's why selecting keywords is so important

If you don't select the right keywords to include in your title, subtitle, and the seven keyword boxes, the Amazon search engine won't find your book when people search for books about your topic.

And if the Amazon search engine doesn't find your book, no one will ever know it exists.

It's not only crucial that Amazon finds your book and indexes it for the keywords and phrases you select, but it's also vital that your book ranks high in the search. Here are the facts.

27% of the people who search for a keyword or phrase will click on the book in the #1 position of the search results.

12% will click on the book in the #2 position, and 7% will click on the book listed in the #5 position. In other words, if you can't get your book ranked near the top of the listings, you will not get many sales from keyword searches.

Therefore, go after keywords and phrases for which you can rank #1 or as close to #1 as possible. That's where the money is.

Ranking #1 for a search phrase that gets only 300 searches a month is way better than ranking #25 for a phrase that gets 5,000 searches a month.

So, the first thing you need to do when you start to write a book is select the 10 to 15 keyword phrases for your book that get a reasonable number of searches a month and have a good chance of ranking high.

When I use the term "keyword," I could mean a single word, a two or three-word phrase, or a long-tail phrase with many words.

You'll use your most important keywords in your title and subtitle. Then, use your less important keywords and keyword phrases in the seven keyword boxes (or slots, as they are sometimes called). I'll talk more about the seven keyword slots later.

In addition to selecting the right keywords, there are three other things that are important to have a successful and profitable book—the title, subtitle, and cover but you can't write a good title or subtitle until you know what keywords to use. And you can't design a cover until you have a title and subtitle. So, let's get started and select those all-important keywords.

Most writers wait until they're submitting their book to Amazon for publication, and then, when the submission form asks them to enter their seven keywords in the keyword boxes, that's the first time they give any thought to what their keywords should be. That's a major mistake.

Here are two important points about keywords

1. Don't waste your time optimizing your book for keywords no one is searching for.

2. Don't select keywords that are so competitive you won't stand a chance of beating out the books that have targeted those keywords and already have hundreds (and in some cases thousands) of reviews. For example, you could never rank high for the word *diet*. The world is way too competitive. The phrase *"Mediterranean diet"* is less competitive but still way too competitive for a new author. Maybe you could rank high for a phrase such as a Mediterranean diet for two or a Mediterranean diet for frozen meals.

But you don't want to guess. You need a way to know which keyword phrases you have a good chance of ranking high for and whether they will be profitable. I'll explain that later in this chapter, but first, let's discuss how to use keywords.

How to use your keywords

You need to include your most important keywords in your title or subtitle.

I'll talk about how to write a killer title and subtitle in the following chapters, but first, you have to come up with the best keywords for your book.

There's no advantage to using a keyword more than once. If a keyword is in your title or subtitle, don't include it in one of your seven keyword boxes. It doesn't hurt anything; it's just a waste of one of the keyword boxes.

Now that you know how important keywords are and how and where to use them, let's get on with how to determine your most important ones. If you do this right, you're well on your way to having a successful and profitable book.

Take the time to systematically select the most searched-for keywords and phrases you can rank high for, and you'll be way ahead of most writers.

How to find the best keywords for your book without spending any money

Before we get into the exact step-by-step process that I use to find profitable keywords for my books, let's talk about what makes a profitable keyword in the first place.

Your keywords should be words or phrases that meet these three conditions:

1. People type it into the Amazon search box

2. It doesn't have a lot of competition

3. People spend money after searching for the phrase

Now that you know what qualifies as a good keyword or phrase let me show you how to find these keywords and phrases without spending any money. Then, I'll also show you how you can make the process easier and faster if you have a little money in your budget to invest in tools.

There are three common ways writers find keywords

#1. Intuition or gut feeling.

#2. Manual methods.

#3. Using one of the keyword tools.

I've used all three of these techniques. They all work, and I will go into the details of all three techniques so you can decide which one you want to use.

#1. Intuition or gut feeling. Using this technique is how many writers come up with their keywords. It's how almost all beginning authors come up with their keywords (if they even bother to select them). You can come up with some reasonably good keywords using this method, but you'll never know if you've found the best ones.

There are two big problems with this technique:

1. You won't think of all of the good keywords.

2. Some of the keywords you come up with won't be profitable for you. That's because some of the keywords you think of will get a lot of searches, but you (as a new author) won't have a chance to rank high for those popular keywords. A keyword that gets a lot of searches but is so competitive that only the big boys will rank for it is not a word you should go after.

Since you know your topic, I'm sure you have a pretty good idea about some keywords and phrases, but run them through the tests described in the manual method or use one of the keyword tools described below to ensure they're profitable.

You may find that some of the keywords you came up with won't be profitable, and you shouldn't use them. They won't be profitable if not many people are searching for them, and they won't be profitable if they're so popular that you won't have a chance of ranking high for them.

#2. The manual methods. There are several ways to find keywords manually. I'll describe the best ones here. These techniques are free, and they all work. I've used them for many of my books, but they can be time-consuming. With these methods, you'll manually find keywords that people are searching for and that other authors are using. Then, you'll need to check to see if they'll be profitable.

Techniques to manually find the best keywords

First, put your browser in **Incognito mode** so none of your previous searches will influence the search results you see. **This step is crucial.**

If you're using the Chrome browser, click on the three vertical dots in the right corner at the top of your screen to put your browser in Incognito mode. Then, in the dropdown menu, click on **the New Incognito window.** Or, if you're using Windows, you can type Ctrl+Shift+N.

Manual Keyword Technique #1: Start by searching Google for the phrase "Amazon Bestsellers Nonfiction."

Then click on "Amazon Bestsellers Nonfiction," which is usually the first listing on the list that shows up.

Amazon doesn't show many of their 17,000 categories on the left-hand side, but you should select the category from that short list that best fits your topic, such as Arts & Photography, Crafts, Hobbies & Home, Self-Help, etc.

Click on that category and look at the top 100 books on the bestsellers list. Look for keywords (or phrases) in each of the top 100 book titles and subtitles and write them on your list.

(Note that many nonfiction books don't have useable keywords in the title or subtitle. That's great news for you. It makes competing with them much easier.)

For example, Stephen Covey's popular book *First Things First* doesn't have a subtitle, and there is not a single word in the title that I would consider a keyword.

Manual Keyword Technique #2: Go to Amazon and search in the "All" category. Enter a keyword phrase you think the potential buyer will be searching for, and Amazon will bottom-fill the keywords and keyword phrases most searched for. The most searched-for phrases will be at the top of the list.

Use long-tailed keyword phrases and NOT single keywords. Words such as diet, exercise, travel, retirement, sales, marketing, investing, etc., get a ton of searches, but as a new, unknown author, you can't hope that your book would rank high for one of these popular keywords. You have to go after the descriptive but less searched-for keyword phrases. This is important to remember.

Go to Amazon and enter your general niche search term, hit "Enter," and at the top of the page, Amazon will show you the total number of search results for that word or phrase.

When doing this exercise, enter your general niche search term in the "All" category, not the "Book" category.

The reason you want to search in the "All" category is that when most people search for a book, they search in the "All" category instead of the "Book" category most of the time because that's the way the screen comes up. People don't bother to change the category. Since most people search in the "All" category, you want to search that way, too, so you'll see the same results they see.

My results have consistently shown that the keyword phrases that will get my book ranked on the first page of the search results are the ones that have fewer than 1,000 searches in the "All" category.

Later, when you have several reviews, you can change keywords in your seven keyword boxes and go after more competitive terms. You can't change your book's title or subtitle, but that's okay. You can go after the more competitive keywords by putting them in your keyword boxes.

When you type in your general niche keyword or keyword phrase, Amazon will also list other search phrases. These are the phrases that people are searching for. The words and phrases at the top of the list are the most searched for, and they are listed in descending order based on the number of times the phrase has been searched for.

Add each of these keyword phrases that apply to your book to your spreadsheet. Then, enter each search phrase into the Amazon search bar and search to see what other keyword phrases show up.

When you click on a phrase at the top of the page, Amazon will take you to a page showing the number of searches for that phrase. Enter this number into your spreadsheet and then move on to the next phrase on the list. In other words, as it says on the shampoo bottle, lather, rinse, and repeat.

If the search results number is less than 1,000, you will have a good chance of appearing on the first page of the search results. If the search results number is below 100 searches a month, that indicates there might not be enough interest in that topic to be profitable for you. **Find keywords and phrases that get between 100 and 1,000 searches a month.**

I wouldn't suggest going after keywords that get much more than 1,000 searches per month unless you plan to run an Amazon ad campaign, and I don't recommend spending money on an ad campaign for your first book. I've never run an Amazon ad campaign.

After going through all of these steps, you should have a long list of keywords that fit your topic and get a lot of searches. Here's a way to find even more keyword phrases.

Manual Keyword Technique #3: When you've found a lot of phrases that you think will be a good search phrase for your book, work with them some more by adding each letter of the alphabet to the end of the phrase and see what other phrases Amazon comes up with.

For example, "Mediterranean diet a," then "Mediterranean diet b," etc. As you do this, look at all the phrases that come up and see if any of them would work for your topic.

Click on any new phrases you like and repeat the process using the alphabet technique. This will surely give you more keyword suggestions than you could have imagined and many keyword phrases that you would never have thought of on your own.

How to evaluate the profitability of keywords

You need to determine which 10 to 15 keywords or phrases on your long list will be the most profitable.

The three factors to look at when determining the profitability of a keyword are:

- **The average BSR (Bestseller Rank),** anything less than 200,000, is excellent. This indicates that a lot of books are being sold.

- **The number of audiobooks listed for that keyword**, less than 100, is excellent.

- **The number of audiobooks with over 50 reviews.**

Let me explain how to use these three indicators and why I like to look at audiobook data.

Check the average **BSR (Bestseller Ranking)** for the 20 books you see on the first page when you search for a keyword phrase. (You can manually find the BSR number by clicking on the book and going to its Amazon Detail Page. If the free DS Amazon Quick View Chrome Extension is installed, you will see the BSR at the bottom of the book's listing.) If you see three or more books on the first page with a BSR of 400,000 or lower, that's a reliable indicator that the search phrase targets buyers, and that's a keyword you want to consider seriously.

Any BSR average for the top 20 bestsellers below 200,000 is good. The lower, the better. A BSR of less than 200,000 means that there's a lot of demand.

Audiobook search results. Note: I like to use audiobook data to do my research because if the audiobook version of the book is selling well, for sure, the eBook and printed versions will be selling well.

Here's how to use audiobook data

- **Find out how many audiobooks have been published about your topic.** Go to Audible.com, and in the box that says, "Find your next great listen," type in your keyword and click "Enter." Above the first listing, you will see 1–20 of xxx. The xxx is the total number of audiobooks using your selected keyword phrase. Anything less than 100 is excellent. The fewer books that are available, the better. But if there are no books or only one or two available, maybe there's no interest in the topic. You might want to reconsider publishing a book on that topic. This is especially true if several keyword phrases show no audiobooks have been published about that topic.

- **How strong is the competition?** The strength of the competition is easy to find. Check to see how many of the top 20 audiobooks (sorted by best-selling) have 50 or more reviews. If an audiobook has only five or ten reviews, the book will not be much competition for you. On the other hand, a book with 100 or 200 reviews will be much harder for you to compete with. There's a lot of gray area between those numbers, but I like to use the numbers 50 and below as a reasonable number I can compete with.

There's one more point to consider. Amazon favors newer books, so if most of the books you'll be competing with are old, that's good news for you. Amazon will consider them outdated, making it easier for you to compete.

Here's where you will have to use some judgment. If 10 of the top 20 best-selling audiobooks have 50 or more reviews, or if there are five or more books with 200 reviews, then you'll know that it's going to be hard for you to compete. If there are two or three books with 500 to over 1,000 reviews, then you know that you would be competing with the big boys, and you should probably select a different keyword.

Look at the situation from your standpoint as a book buyer. If you were looking to buy a book on a topic and one book you were considering had 500 reviews, and another had five, which one would you buy? Even if one book had 200 reviews and one had 10, you would probably still go with the book with 200 reviews.

The techniques I've described show you how to manually find the most profitable keywords for your book. They work and are free, but they take a lot of time.

Describing the manual methods for finding keywords was a long section. Now, let me tell you about the third way of finding keywords: by using a keyword tool.

#3. Use one of the keyword tools. There are several keyword tools. They all make the keyword selection process easier, faster, and more thorough. Some are free, some are low-cost, and some are a little more expensive.

Here's the tool I use now to find the best keywords for my books

In the past, I've used all three of the manual methods described previously to find keywords for the books I've written. But the way I do it now is to use a keyword tool. I've tested most of the keyword tools on the market.

You don't have to grind all of this out. You can use a tool called **Publisher Rocket** to do all of the heavy lifting for you.

Below is my affiliate link to the **Publisher Rocket** website.

aLaptopLife.com/rocket

Here's a brief explanation of how to use this tool and what it will do for you.

With this tool, I can easily find the **competitive score**, **average monthly earnings**, and the **estimated number of Amazon searches/month** of the keywords I'm considering. With this information, I can quickly and confidently find the most valuable keywords for my book.

You can find all this information manually, but this tool is much faster and easier.

How to use the Publisher Rocket tool

If you decide to use this tool, videos on the company's website and on YouTube will show you how to use it and how to get the most out of it quickly. Below is a brief overview of how to use the tool.

Start by clicking on the "Keyword Search" button. Then, choose whether you want keywords for a printed book, an eBook, or an audiobook. I go through the steps for both the eBook and the printed book. Most of the keywords are the same for the eBook and the printed book, but sometimes there are slight differences.

Then click "**Go Get Em Rocket**." The program will give you a list of keyword phrases matching your entered keyword. Go through the list and click the "**Analyze**" button for the keywords you think would be a good choice for your book from the list the program has suggested.

Next, look at the "**Competitive Score**." The Competitive Score is a number between 1 and 100, with 1 being no competition at all and 100 being extremely competitive. A score below 25 is super easy to compete with, and a score above 75 is challenging. Since you're a new author, I recommend trying to find keywords with a Competitive Score below 50. Below 40 would be even better.

Next, look at the column that shows the "**Average Monthly Earnings**" for that keyword. This is the average amount each of the top five books that use that keyword is earning a month. I'm usually not interested in keywords earning less than $100 a month. I generally like to find keywords making $200 or more a month. And, of course, keywords earning more than $1,000 a month are much better.

The next thing to look at is the number of people who have typed that exact keyword phrase into Amazon.

To summarize, for the keywords the program has found for you, look at the numbers in the following three columns.

Competitive Score—Below 50 is good, and below 25 is really good.

Average Monthly Earnings—$100 minimum. $500 to $1,000 is a lot better.

Estimated Amazon Searches/Month—Select keywords that get greater than 100 per month.

I pick out the 10 to 15 keywords with the best combination of a reasonably low Competitive Score, high

Average Monthly Earnings, and a high number of Amazon Searches/Month.

You don't have to write everything down when you find all this information. Click on "Export," and the program will export all of the data to a spreadsheet for you.

The program is simple to use.

I select one of the best keywords or phrases to include in my book's title, one or two for the subtitle, and seven more for Amazon's keyword boxes.

Sometimes, instead of including keywords in the subtitle, I use a powerful phrase to help sell the book. If I can come up with a keyword or two that helps sell the book, including them in the subtitle is even better.

Deciding on a subtitle is where you get to be creative and use your judgment.

If you want to do more research before making your final selection on your keywords, click the Competition button on the right side of the chart in the Publisher Rocket program. It will bring up the 20 books on Amazon's first page that you will be competing against for that keyword. This will show you a ton of information about the books you will be competing against.

For example, do they have the keyword in their title or subtitle? What are their daily sales and their monthly sales? What is their BSR (Bestseller Rank)? And you'll find additional information to help you learn more about the books you will be competing against. For example, you can see the covers of your competitors' books.

The program also provides information to help you select the Categories for your book. (I'll talk about how to choose categories in Chapter 12.)

Below is a link to the **Publisher Rocket** website.

aLaptopLife.com/rocket

This is an affiliate link, and it's the only time I've ever placed an affiliate link in any of my 20+ books. I believe in it that much. I don't gush over many things, but I'll make an exception for this program. If you're going to write a book, this tool is worth its weight in gold.

Check out their program description and scroll down to the button where it says, "See Rocket in Action." Watch some of the videos and see if you think this program will be worth the cost to you.

The two features of the program I use the most to help me find the best keywords are:

#1. Keyword Research

#2. Competition Analyzer

With all the work you'll put into writing and creating your book, don't get lazy and neglect to give your book the best chance of success by failing to select the most profitable keywords for eBooks and printed books. Sometimes, the best keywords for each type of book will be the same, but many times, choosing the same keywords will not be the best thing to do.

Note: The title and subtitle have to be the same for your print book and your eBook, but the keywords you put in the seven keyword slots can be different. Also, you can't change the title or subtitle after the book is published, but you can change the keywords in your seven keyword slots at any time. Sometimes, you'll want to change some of your keyword phrases and go after some of the more competitive phrases after you get more reviews.

To summarize: To own Publisher Rocket, you have to make a one-time investment of $97 for lifetime use. You get lifetime upgrades when you own this program. In late 2021, they came out with a new version that added several new and valuable features. Then, again, in late 2022, they came out with another upgrade.

The Publisher Rocket keyword tool requires an investment, but I use it all the time and find it well worth the money because it saves me so much time.

In addition to helping you find keywords, it's also a valuable marketing tool to help you learn about your competition and which categories would be the most profitable for your book. The program shows you how many sales a day would be required to rank #1 and #10 in each category. And it shows you the categories in which each book you will be competing with is listed.

I'll discuss selecting categories in Chapter 12 and marketing your book in Chapter 16.

You can find keywords for your book without spending any money. The main purpose of using a keyword tool is to save you time and make the process easier. You'll also likely find more profitable keywords when using a keyword tool.

If you want to make money with your book, don't go with the intuition or gut feeling method of finding keywords. Use one of the manual methods I've described or the Publisher Rocket tool.

There are some other free and low-cost keyword tools available, but I haven't listed them in this book because I've tried them and found them to be frustrating to use, and I don't recommend them.

Use your keywords correctly

- Don't stuff too many keywords into your title. Keep it clean, and don't confuse the Amazon search engine. Don't try to rank high for a ton of keywords. Keep your title short if you can. (I didn't do that with this book.)

- Place your best keyword near the front of your

title. Using your most powerful keyword phrase in the title is better.

- Then, place your next two best keywords in your subtitle near the front if possible. Placing keywords near the front of the title and subtitle is called front-end loading. Amazon values this technique when ranking books for a particular keyword.

- Amazon does not index the words in the description, so including keywords there will not help your Amazon ranking. However, Google does index the words in your description.

How to get the most benefit from your seven keyword boxes

You are allowed 50 characters (including spaces) in each keyword box. Should you add keywords to take advantage of all 50 allowed characters, or should you only place one keyword or keyword phrase in each box? The simple answer is that you should do some of both.

Amazon won't index your book for a keyword that's not included in your title, subtitle, or one of the keyword boxes, so the more keywords you have in the boxes, the more words Amazon will index your book for.

That all sounds good, but the more words you include in a box, the more diluted Amazon considers the keyword. In other words, if you have a lot of keywords in a box, your book will be indexed for all of these words, but you probably won't rank high for any of them.

Here's how you can have the best of both worlds. Use three or four of your keyword boxes for your most important keywords or phrases (that were not used in your title or subtitle). There is no advantage to repeating keywords already used in the title or subtitle.

Repeating a word in a different phrase is okay and even helpful. For example, one of your keyword phrases might be "Skills for young entrepreneurs," and another might be "Secrets of experienced entrepreneurs."

Then, use your other boxes and fill them with niche-specific keywords that fit your topic but don't get as many searches as your most important ones. Put a space between each word or phrase but no punctuation.

For the other keywords, use words that describe the problem your book will solve, the benefit the reader will receive, who the book is for (men, women, retired people, business owners, etc.), or synonyms for your keywords.

It's not the purpose of your keyword boxes to describe your book. The purpose of the words in your keyword boxes is to include words that a prospective buyer might use when searching for a book like yours. So, don't use words like amazing, beautiful, or informative. These words might describe your book, but no one will type these words when searching for a book.

Don't use irrelevant keywords. Using these words will dilute the value of your important keywords. Using unrelated words could also confuse Amazon about what your book is about.

Use keyword phrases with three words or more in your seven keyword boxes. As an unknown author with your first book, your book will not rank high for any single word (or even two words) in most cases. Words and phrases such as diet, make money, lose weight, etc., are not words or phrases you should go after initially.

Later, when you get a lot of reviews, you might try changing some of your keywords and try to rank high for the more popular single keywords or keyword phrases.

One last point—include keywords in some chapter titles where they fit.

After you have selected a list of your most profitable keywords, when you get to Chapter 6 about writing your Table of Contents, use several of your keywords in the titles of your chapters if they fit, but don't make the titles sound like you're stuffing them with keywords. You want to be sure to discuss the topics of the keywords in your book. Having chapters about your most important keywords is one certain way to accomplish this.

Bonus technique for increasing your Amazon rankings

If you have friends you know who are going to buy your book, instead of sending them the link to go to Amazon to buy your book, tell them to go to Amazon and search for the keyword phrase you give them. Tell them to use this method to find your book and buy it. Every time this happens, it tells Amazon that your book is a good fit for that keyword phrase, and that helps to raise your ranking for that keyword phrase.

Don't get overwhelmed

This chapter is long, but selecting the best keywords for your book is the most crucial factor that will determine how successful and profitable your book will be.

After you finish reading this book, come back and reread this chapter when you're ready to select your keywords. There are way too many details to comprehend if you read it only once.

Don't worry if all of this seems overwhelming. The techniques will be easier to understand when you start using them.

Look on the bright side. Since going through these steps to select the best keywords is a little bit difficult and time-consuming, most of your competitors won't bother. Since they won't do the work, and you will, that makes it easier for you to rank higher for more keywords, and, likewise, you'll sell more books.

After you've selected your most profitable keyword phrases, move on to Chapter 4 and come up with your title and subtitle. Then, you're ready to start writing your book.

When you use the techniques described in this chapter to find the best and most profitable keywords for your book, you won't have to wonder whether you selected the right ones. You can be confident that you have the very best keywords on the planet for your book.

If you don't select the most profitable keywords and phrases for your book, you won't have a chance of having a profitable book. It's that simple.

There are several options presented in this chapter for finding the best keywords for your book, but my recommendation (if your budget allows it) is to invest in the **Publisher Rocket** tool. (It works with both PC and Mac computers.) You can learn more about it at this affiliate link.

aLaptopLife.com/rocket

One final point: I can't stress enough how important the keyword selection process is for having a profitable book.

The main takeaway from this chapter: You don't want to put a lot of effort into writing a book that won't sell well because you targeted the wrong keywords. Selecting the best and most profitable keywords for your book is the most important thing you can do to have a profitable book.

Find your book's best and most profitable keywords and phrases before you develop a title, subtitle, and book cover.

Chapter 4

Write a Title and Subtitle That Will Hook the Reader

"If my doctor told me I had only six minutes to live, I wouldn't brood. I'd type a little faster."

~ Isaac Asimov

The title and subtitle of your book are two of the five most important factors that will determine the success of your book. The other three are the cover design, the keywords you optimize for, and your Amazon detail page description. I'll talk about all of these in later chapters.

The title and subtitle of your book have two primary purposes.

#1. Have keywords so the Amazon search engine will find your book.

#2. Then, hook the reader and make them want to buy your book. Convince them that your book has the solution to their problem.

The title should be short if possible, but make it longer if needed to get the point across. Note that the title of this book is not short, but I didn't see any words I wanted to omit. You want the title to be short enough to fit on the page and be in large enough text to be easy to read when someone is looking at the small thumbnail image Amazon shows.

The subtitle can be longer. The subtitles are not easy to read for most books when looking at Amazon's thumbnail image. That's okay.

You can include additional related keywords in Amazon's seven keyword boxes but put your most important keywords and keyword phrases in the title and subtitle.

You want your book title and subtitle to make your book look like it was written by a professional authority figure on the topic.

Note: Audible (the publisher of audiobooks) looks for exact keyword matches in the title and subtitle. Amazon will look for variations of the keywords you use.

Your book can't be about everything. It can't even cover everything about your primary topic. Your book needs to drill down and be about the one finite point of your subject.

In other words, your book can't be about "Diet." It should be about one kind of diet or about one aspect of dieting. Your book can't be all things to all people. Don't try to stuff too many keywords in your title and subtitle.

Here's the title of this book:

How to Write a Nonfiction Book and Publish It on Amazon

And here is the subtitle:

A Complete Step-By-Step Beginner's Guide

to Writing and Publishing

Your First Book—at Zero Cost

This title and subtitle clearly describe the problems this book will solve.

Note: This title and subtitle are longer than I would have liked, but this topic is hard to describe in fewer words.

This title and subtitle speak to people who want to write and publish a book on Amazon but don't know where to start and don't have a big budget to spend on the project.

Having keywords in your title and subtitle will help people find your book. But to make people want to buy your book, your title has to convince them that your book has the solution to their problem.

The one thing people judge a book by is the title. Your title must be intriguing and convince the reader that this book has the answer to his questions and will tell him what he wants to know. In other words, the title and subtitle should convince the person considering buying your book that this book has the solution to their problem.

Use words that rank high as keywords or search terms, but don't just stuff keywords into your title. Your title and subtitle should make it clear that your book will solve the potential reader's problem.

There's no advantage to using a word in your subtitle if it's already used in your title. It's a waste of valuable space to use a word more than once in your title or subtitle.

And from a search point of view, there's no advantage to using different versions of a word. If you've used the singular version of a word, there's no reason to use the plural version. For example, if you've used the word dog, there's no advantage from a search perspective to using the word dogs. If you've used train, there's no need to use the word training.

How to come up with a title that will hook your reader

Don't write one version of your title and get set on it. Write at least a dozen versions of your title and two or three dozen variations would be even better. Every time you sit down to write, read over your list of titles and see what you think of them and what new versions you can come up with.

When you're reasonably sure of the title and subtitle, it's time to design the cover.

I often change the subtitle and sometimes even the title of a book while writing it. For example, I added the words *at zero cost* to the subtitle of this book after I started writing it. I had already paid for the cover, but since it was designed in layers, it was easy to make the change. My cover designer didn't even charge me.

Don't get too cute with your title. The most important thing you can do with your title is to have it include an exact keyword phrase that people are searching for.

This is not always possible, and you don't want your title to sound like you're doing "keyword stuffing." Instead, you want it to sound natural.

If you're a famous writer, you can get by with a title that doesn't have keywords. If you have a keyword-rich subtitle, you could get by without keywords in your title, but it's still better to have highly searched-for keywords in your title.

For example, the book *Rich Dad Poor Dad* is still #1 in the Personal Finance category even though it was published years ago, and it doesn't have any keywords in the title. It does have a few keywords in the subtitle, but not what I would consider the best ones for the book's topic.

You want your title to clearly say what benefit the reader will receive when reading your book. The book title should state a solution to someone's problem.

Here are some book title examples that make it clear what problem the book will solve

How to pay off your student loan in three years—regardless of how much you owe.

You could omit the "How to" part of the phrase and have a title like this.

Pay off your student loan debt in three years—regardless of how much you owe.

Your title should talk about the outcome the reader wants to achieve.

What would you promise in your title if you had godlike powers and could deliver any benefit or outcome? Come up with a benefit that your book really can provide. Use that as your title.

Here are the two most important things that make a great book title.

#1. You need a title with a keyword phrase someone is searching for.

#2. You need a title that promises the outcome the reader wants.

Do these two things, and you will have a successful and profitable book title.

A lot of books have bad titles. Many writers try to get cute with their book titles. Do an excellent job of creating your book title, and you will be way ahead of your competition.

Don't use the titles of best-selling books as examples for your title. Many of these books don't have keywords in their titles. The books may sell well because the author has a large following, is well known in the industry, or promotes his book through advertising or other means than through Amazon searches. You don't have that option. You will be relying almost exclusively on Amazon search results to find buyers for your book.

Your book title needs to make it crystal clear what your book is about and what benefits the reader will get by reading it.

The purpose of your nonfiction book is to provide a solution to someone's problem. Always keep that point in mind. The title must convince the reader that your book delivers the solution to their problem.

Your title should be a hook and should invoke an emotion.

In fiction books, the title often doesn't make any sense until after you've read the book. Then, you can realize where the title came from.

For example, the books *Gone With the Wind* and *To Kill a Mockingbird* are two popular novels that have sold millions, and after you've read the books, you understand where the title came from and what it means. But before you read the book, the title tells you nothing about what the book is about. You don't even have a clue.

When writing a nonfiction book, you don't have the luxury of having this kind of title. Your title has to hook the potential reader and tell them precisely what the book is about and what they'll get out of reading it.

The subtitle doesn't have to be a hook. The subtitle allows you to use more keywords and lets you more clearly explain how the book will solve the reader's problem.

Put effort into coming up with a good subtitle. Don't just think of something off of the top of your head. And don't be afraid to change the title or subtitle while writing your book.

Remember that although you can change your book's content after it's published, you can't change the title or subtitle, so make sure you have a killer title and subtitle before you publish your book.

To Summarize: You want a powerful title and subtitle, but you don't want it to read like you were stuffing it with keywords. Accomplishing this is not always easy to do, so plan on putting a lot of time into writing and tweaking your title and subtitle.

Don't just write one title and subtitle. Write a dozen or two. Decide on a title and subtitle before you start writing your book, but feel free to make changes as you write it. I read my title and subtitle every time I sit down to write, and I almost always make some changes before I finish the book.

One final note: Your subtitle does not have to be included on the cover of your book. If it's long, it will be so small that it will be hard to read on the tiny thumbnail image that Amazon displays. Amazon will show the subtitle next to the title on the Product Detail page, and they will index the words. If you are going to sell your book in a bookstore, a small subtitle on the cover would be okay. I always include my subtitle on the cover.

If your subtitle has two phrases, place a dash between them. If you place them on different lines, they will be easy to read, but Amazon will read them as one confusing sentence and delist your book. I learned that the hard way.

The main takeaway from this chapter: Start with a great title and subtitle, and you will be well on your way to having a successful book. Developing a perfect title and subtitle is challenging, but you can do it. Review your title and subtitle often while writing your book, and don't be afraid to make changes.

Chapter 5

How to Create a Killer Book Cover—Including the Back Cover

"Every writer I know has trouble writing."

~ Joseph Heller

We've all heard the statement, "Don't judge a book by its cover." It may be good advice, but not many people follow it. Almost everyone initially judges a book by looking at its cover.

Of all new books sold worldwide (both eBooks and printed books), 65% are sold by Amazon. I assume that's how you plan to sell your book.

There are 6,000 new books a day being published on Amazon, so how do you get yours noticed?

One thing is for sure: You had better have an eye-catching cover design. Having a wimpy cover on your book is a recipe for disaster. Your title must be large enough to be easily read when someone is looking at the thumbnail image of your book that Amazon posts on their sales page.

It must use an easily read font, not some fancy Gothic or script typestyle, and it must contrast with the background or image of the front cover.

When someone looks at the thumbnail image of your book cover, the title must stand out and be easy to read.

Many writers work on writing their book for months or even years and then, at the last minute, try to come up with a book cover with little thought put into the process. Then they wonder why their book doesn't sell.

I usually have my book cover designed before I write many words of the book. This serves two purposes. First, having the book's cover designed keeps me motivated to continue writing the book. I even temporarily post the cover design at the beginning of my book, so I will see it every time I sit down to write.

Book covers are designed in layers, so it's easy to change the title or subtitle any time before you publish your book. Amazon will allow you to change the cover's design, the book's text, and many other things about your book even after it's published. The only things you can't change are the title and subtitle. They are linked to the ISBN and cannot be changed.

Four ways to design a book cover

Here are the four common ways to get your book cover designed. They range from free to slightly expensive. I've used all four techniques for the more than 20 books I've published.

#1. Design your own cover. With Photoshop or one of the free Scribus, GIMP, or Canva tools, you can design a great-looking cover yourself. The best part about this technique is that it's free. You can go to Pexels.com or Pixabay.com and download one of their almost two million high-quality free images to use on your book cover.

Photoshop is a great program, but it's not free. If you don't already own Photoshop, you can do the same thing with GIMP, which is an open-source, free program for graphics editing and image manipulation.

#2. Have a graphic designer at Fiverr.com design a cover for you. I've used some of their designers to design book covers for me. They do a good job, and the price is usually about $25 to $50 for both the eBook and the printed book version. Keep in mind that the designers can't finish the design for the cover for the printed version of your book until you finish writing the book and have it formatted. They have to know how many pages the book will have so they will know how thick to make the spine.

The more information you can give the designer about what you want your book cover to look like, the better job they will do for you. You may even want to tell them which image to use and maybe even what font you want to use on the cover.

Or you may just give them free rein and see what they come up with. I've done it both ways. You can have them make changes after they send you a design. You can tell them to change the color of the text, make the title or subtitle larger, etc. Be sure to tell your designer that you want the title to be large and easy to read and not to use a fancy, hard-to-read font.

#3. Use a pre-designed book cover. GoOnWrite.com is a company I've used to design two book covers. The covers were already designed. I just selected the design I liked, and he changed the title and subtitle on the cover to my title and subtitle. Look at the hundreds of pre-designed covers he offers and see if you find one you like. They are priced at $40 to $50 for both an eBook cover and the front and back cover of the printed version of your book. Most of his covers seem better suited for fiction books, but you can find some for nonfiction. I did.

Here's the link to his list of pre-designed book covers.

https://www.GoOnWrite.com/

#4. Have a professional custom design your book cover. This is the technique I've used for my last three books. This option is more expensive than the other options described. Still, since I firmly believe that the cover of the book has a lot to do with how well it sells, I usually spend the extra money on a professionally designed cover.

It's not a necessity that you have a professional design your cover. My two best-selling books have covers where I picked out the photo and font I wanted to use. Then, I had a designer from Fiverr.com do the cover designs.

The back cover

An eBook doesn't have a back cover. If your book were primarily going to be sold in bookstores, the purpose of the back cover would be to convince the person holding your book to go ahead and buy it.

But since your book will be sold on Amazon, the potential buyer may not even see the back cover until after he has bought the book. The back cover won't help your book sales very much, though it may help in a few cases. So, what's the main purpose of the back cover?

I use the back cover to promote my other books. Since I have almost 30 other books, I only have room for showing a thumbnail picture of some of them.

If you only have one or two other books, you can include a picture and a brief description of them.

If this is your first book, remember that you can (and you should) go back and change the back cover as soon as you publish another book.

If this is your first book, use the back cover to talk about yourself and mention that you will soon have other books published.

There are four primary purposes of the back cover of a printed book

1. **Use it to sell your other books or courses.** Or tease about your future books that will be coming out soon. And remember that you can change your back cover later when you write another book. Showing the covers of your other books is a great way to help sell your other books on the topic, as well as helping to establish yourself as an expert in the field. Even if your other books are not on the same subject, having pictures of them on the back cover will help establish you as an accomplished writer and still help sell your other books.

2. **Persuade the buyer to read your book**. You might think this is unnecessary, but many people buy books and never read them or don't finish

reading them. How many books do you have that you haven't read? You're not likely to get a positive review from a buyer who hasn't read your book.

3. **Promote yourself.** Include an "About the Author" blurb and blow your own horn. Including your picture on the back cover will help the reader feel like they know you. When a reader feels like they know you, they're more likely to leave a review and buy your future books. It will also encourage the reader to read the book and prevent buyer's remorse. One of the reasons to write a book is to help establish yourself as an expert on the book's topic. Make use of the back cover to help accomplish this.

4. **Create excitement to get people to buy your book.** Yes, a few potential buyers will click on the little picture of your book's back cover and look at it when they're on Amazon considering your book. If you can get them to read your description, you're one step closer to convincing them to click on the "Add to cart" button and buy your book.

How to write a compelling back cover blurb

You want to ensure your blurb clearly explains what the book is about. You don't want someone to buy your book and then find out it's not about what they thought it was. You're likely to get a bad review if the reader is disappointed. Your back cover blurb should be clear and honest.

Things to include on your back cover

- Include two or three of your best quotes or reviews about how fantastic the book is. You can get reviews before your book is published by sending a copy of your manuscript to influential people and asking them to give you a quote or comment about the book that you can use to promote it. You'll be surprised how easy it is to get some of these endorsements if you just ask for them.

- What you include on the back cover will depend on what you have. Do you have endorsements or quotes you can use? Do you have other books you've written? You can change your book cover at any time, so after you write your second book, consider adding information and a picture of it on your back cover.

- In the bottom right corner, you'll include your barcode if you're supplying your own or leave a space for Amazon to insert a barcode if they are providing one. I always provide my own barcode.

- Your book cover designer (maybe that's you) will also design the back cover. You'll write the text and supply pictures (such as pictures of other books, etc.). A lot of time, the background of the back cover will be a wraparound of the photo used on the front cover.

Five more things to go on the back cover

1. Your best endorsement—hopefully from a well-known person in your field. Later, after the book is published, if you get a better endorsement or one from a famous person, you can add it or replace the one you have.

2. A powerful opening sentence that describes your book.

3. Next, use the heading "Discover how to" and then list five to seven (an odd number) short one-sentence bullet points talking about the benefits the reader will get from reading your book.

4. A closing wrap-up sentence.

5. Finally, have an "About the Author" heading and then one paragraph about yourself—your background, your education, and maybe something about your family and dog (if you have one). Potential readers want to feel like they know you. Including a small picture on the left side of your About the Author paragraph will help readers

feel like they know you.

6. Here's a bonus point: If you have a website (and you should), include a link to it in the bottom left corner of the back cover or as the last line of your About the Author paragraph.

With a well-designed front and back cover, you're well on your way to having a best-selling book.

One final point: If you include an image of your cover in your eBook when you upload it, be sure it's a compressed version. I like to keep this image below about 200KB. If you don't, Amazon could charge you up to a dollar as a digital delivery fee because Amazon charges 15¢ per MB. This is described in detail in Chapter 10 when I'm talking about how to add photos to your book.

The main takeaway from this chapter: People do judge a book by its cover, so be sure to put the time and effort into getting an attention-grabbing cover for your book and have it designed before you do much writing of the book. You don't want your cover design to be a last-minute, rushed job or afterthought. You have (or will) put a lot of effort into writing your book. Put effort into getting a stunning cover that will make your book sales skyrocket.

Chapter 6

Write a Table of Contents That Will Sell Your Book

"I always kept two books in my pocket: one to read, one to write in."

~ Robert Louis Stevenson

Your table of contents should serve two purposes. First, it's your outline, keeping you on track and ensuring you don't leave anything out.

If you were to write a novel, you would need to have a detailed outline (either on paper or in your head), but with a nonfiction book, it's a whole different world. My table of contents is my outline.

The second purpose of your table of contents is to help sell your book. Many people will look at it when deciding whether or not to buy your book.

When a potential purchaser of your book is looking at the cover, title, subtitle, and description, many of them will also click on Amazon's "Look inside" button, which is right above the picture of the book. The table of contents is usually one of the pages that Amazon shows.

Take advantage of this fact and make sure your table of contents does an excellent job of selling your book by showing chapter titles that will capture the reader's attention and convince them that your book has the solution to their problem. In other words, the table of contents should make them want to read your book.

You'll need at least eight to 10 chapters. I usually have 15 to 20. I like shorter chapters. Make sure you have chapters covering everything you promised in your title, subtitle, and Introduction.

Your table of contents is your outline, and I often rearrange my chapters. I also add and delete chapters as I'm writing the book. Most of the time, when I sit down to write, I start by reading over the Table of Contents. That's when I sometimes make changes and decide which chapter I want to start writing next. I don't write the chapters in order. I usually jump around and work on the chapters I'm most passionate about first.

That's why sometimes I get close to finishing a book and realize there's a chapter or two that I haven't worked on. That's when I sometimes know I'm not passionate about the subject of that chapter. Sometimes, I decide to delete that chapter and include two or three sentences about that topic in another chapter instead.

Sometimes, when I start to write, I want to pick up where I left off and continue writing on a chapter I was working on. In those cases, I skip reading over the table of contents.

After I write the table of contents, I create a separate page for each chapter with the chapter number and title at the top of the page.

Then, each chapter is ready for me to start adding the text. I usually start by writing the Introduction and then work on the chapters I'm most interested in and passionate about.

By having a page set up in my manuscript for each chapter, I can quickly jump around and add information or notes to any chapter.

Also, when I'm reading or doing research, and I come across information I want to include in my book, I'll jump to the chapter where I think the information should go, and I'll add the information or a note about the topic so I won't forget to include it when I start writing on that chapter.

Note: I change the titles of my chapters a lot as I write my book. When you change the title of a chapter, immediately change the table of contents. Don't leave this as something you will do later. Your proofreader probably wouldn't catch this.

The main takeaway from this chapter: Many potential buyers will use the "Look inside" feature and read your table of contents to see what your book covers and then decide whether to buy it or not, so make sure your table of contents does an excellent job of selling your book.

Chapter 7

Write a Sizzling Description

"The best time to plan a book is while you're doing the dishes."

~ Agatha Christie

After the title and book cover, the description is the next most important thing that will determine how well your book sells.

Your description should not be telling about the book. It should be selling the book. Many authors make a big mistake and try to describe their book in the description. Your description should answer the question, "Should I buy this book?" You need to make your description compelling and exciting, and it should convince the reader that this is the book that has the solution to their problem.

If someone has landed on the Amazon listing for your book, it means you've done a lot of things right (having a good title, subtitle, book cover, and list of keywords). Now, you want your description to get them to take that last step, click on the buy button, and buy your book.

You've worked too hard to get people this far, and you don't want to lose them at this point. Your description has got to convince them to buy the book.

One more step—at the end of the description, go ahead and tell them to click on the Buy button. Say something like, "If it sounds like this book will solve your problem, go ahead and click on the Buy button now."

If you write a poor description, your book won't sell—it's that simple

Readers searching for a nonfiction book are looking for a solution to a problem. Your job as an author is to provide that solution. If you want to sell a lot of books, you'll need a title, subtitle, and description that will convince a reader that your book will deliver the solution they're looking for.

The sad truth is that after spending months (or even years) writing their book, many authors put little effort into writing the description.

Many writers never even think about a description until they start to submit their book on Amazon, and the form comes up and shows them a blank block and tells them to enter their description. They can't proceed with submitting their book until they stop and write one.

So that's what they do. They stop and quickly whip out a description so they can proceed with the process of submitting their book to Amazon to be published.

The book description appears on the Amazon detail page.

Amazon's detail page describes the book to the potential buyer. It's usually the first thing the reader sees after looking at the cover. The detail page has the title and subtitle of the book, the author's name, the category, and, of course, the description.

Your description is one of the important parts of your book's Amazon detail page.

Note: What Amazon calls the detail page is what I would call a sales page. It's a page that's trying to sell the reader on the idea of buying the book.

It's the reader's first chance to learn what your book is about other than what the title and subtitle tell him. If you have a well-written description, it will pique a reader's interest and help convince them that your book has the solution to their problem.

People buy fiction books to be entertained, but they purchase nonfiction books to solve a problem. A good description should convince readers that your book has the solution that will solve their problem.

Your description should start with a powerful hook

A hook is a statement that grabs the reader and pulls him in. You have to grab their attention with the first 30 to 40 words. That's all that Amazon shows on the book detail page before the words "Read more." The reader must click on the words "Read more" before seeing the rest of your description.

That's why the first few words are so important. Use some keywords, but don't keyword stuff. Remember that Amazon doesn't index any of the words in the description.

What would you say if you only had one sentence to sell your book?

Regardless of how powerful and beautifully written your description is, the reader will never see it if your first 30 to 40 words don't hook him and make him want to know more.

Here are some of my favorite hooks

What if I told you . . .?

What if you could . . .?

You could drop the *"what if"* and start your descriptions like the ones shown below.

- Live on $800 a Month

- Travel the World on $1,000 a Month

- Lose Weight without Going on a Diet

Break your description into short paragraphs and use boldface type in a few places.

List benefits as bulleted statements

Showing the benefits the reader will receive by buying your book in a list of bulleted statements makes them stand out and easier to comprehend and understand.

Include endorsements in your description when you have them.

Even before your book is published, you should send the manuscript to anyone you know who is famous or is a noted authority on the topic and ask them for an endorsement. When you get their endorsement, you can include it in your description.

Also, note that you can change the description of your book anytime, so even after it's published, if you get another excellent endorsement, change your description to include the new endorsement.

Be sure to tell the reader why this book is for them. Maybe use a strong positive review to close.

Formatting your description is important

To have a description that people will read, you need to have a bold headline, maybe a little larger than the rest of the text. You'll need to have some bullet points, a few words or phrases in bold, and have your description broken into several short paragraphs.

Don't make your description just one long paragraph. No one will read it.

The purpose of your description is to sell your book, and it can't sell your book if no one reads it.

To format your description to look this way in the old days (before May 21, 2021), you had to format it using HTML codes or use a special program to do it for you.

Now, you no longer have to know how to use HTML codes. Amazon has made it easy for you.

When you go to your bookshelf inside KDP and start to upload your content, you'll scroll down until you get to the description box. Inside the description box, you'll see another small box with the symbols that will allow you to change the formatting of your description.

Paste the description you've previously written into the box. (That's a better way to do it than to try typing it into the box.) Then, use the tools that Amazon provides to make some of your text bold, use numbers or bullets, use headings and subheadings, and change the size of different parts of your text. In other words, make your description easy to read. Most people won't read a long paragraph of text.

A summary of the steps to creating a great description

Here's an easy guide to follow. Start your description with an attention-grabbing hook. Next, explain how your book will solve the reader's problem. Then, list or outline your credibility (why you're qualified to solve their problem), include endorsements if you have them, and finally, close with a call to action (ask the reader to buy the book).

One last point: Include some of the most important keywords in your description. Amazon doesn't look at the words in your description when indexing your book, but Google does. Don't just stuff your keywords into the description. Try to use them in a way that seems natural.

Give a lot of thought to your description and include the text of your description in the manuscript you send to your proofreader so he can check it and make sure it doesn't have any typos or grammatical errors.

The main takeaway from this chapter: Write your description before you do much writing of your book. It shouldn't be an afterthought. Reread it from time to time as you write your book. Keep it in mind and make sure your book delivers on what you have promised in the description. Follow the steps described in this chapter, and you'll have a sizzling description that will boost your sales.

Chapter 8

Now You're Ready to Start Writing—Here's How

"The first draft is just you telling yourself the story."

~ Terry Pratchett

This chapter is long, but it needs to be. It contains a lot of important information you need to understand before you start writing your book. You may want to read it (or parts of it) more than once. Refer back to it from time to time.

I recommend you write your manuscript using MS Word or the free LibreOffice Writer.

When you're a writer, you can't depend on inspiration. You have to rely on dedication and discipline. Peter De Vries put it this way:

"I only write when I'm inspired,
so I see to it that I'm inspired every morning at
nine o'clock."

When you start writing, remember to picture one person and write like you're talking to that person and explaining something to them. Talk "to" them and not "at" them.

Start by writing your Introduction chapter. This chapter mainly tells the reader what they will learn from reading your book.

Your Introduction must be compelling and convince readers that your book will solve their problem.

What is your unique message? This is important. What information, experience, and advice do you have that no one else has?

Your Introduction should speak to the reader. Let them know that you understand their problem and feel their pain.

Also, realize that many potential buyers of your book will click on the "Read sample" button on the Amazon site before deciding to buy it. When they click on that, they'll likely see your table of contents and the first chapter or two, which will be your Introduction and maybe another chapter.

Your Introduction chapter is your chance to convince potential readers that your book will solve their problems. If you can do that, they'll most likely buy your book. That's why I think the Introduction is the most crucial chapter of your book. I usually tweak it several times as I continue writing the book.

Here are some things to ask yourself when you're writing your book

- What problems are other books in your niche talking about or claiming they can solve?

- Use the "Look inside" feature on Amazon and look at the Table of Contents of other books in your niche. What topics are they covering? What are they promising?

- Since conventional wisdom is often wrong, what unique experience or ideas do you have that will allow you to solve the problem in a different way?

- Most importantly—what is your hook? I talked about that in Chapter 4.

More things to consider

- Commit to doing your absolute best work. You don't want to end up with a crappy book. Writing your book fast should NOT be your goal.

- When you write, picture one person you're talking to and explain things to that person. Don't write as if you're talking to a large group of people.

- Your goal should be to move people; don't just entertain and inform them.

- People want a transformation—not information.

- Don't preach. Your goal should be to take the reader by the hand and bring them along with you. Tell them, "I was once where you are" (if really you were).

- Facts tell, and stories sell. (Stories keep the reader engaged and keep them turning the page to see what to do next.)

- You want a killer opening. This is important. I sometimes rewrite or tweak my opening line several times.

How to deal with writer's block

If you find yourself having trouble writing (or experiencing writer's block), most likely, it's because you're trying to explain something just right. In other words, your problem is that you're trying to write the final version instead of the first draft.

Forget about getting your story just right, forget about grammar, and forget about presenting your points in the proper order. Your goal should be to get words on the page. Let your ideas flow, and write what comes to mind. Edit it later. As the famous writer Tom Clancy said, "*Tell the damn story.*"

If you try to write a final version, you'll end up not having many words written. You can't edit and write at the same time.

Always keep in mind that you're not writing a final version. You're writing a rough first draft. If unsure whether to describe a technique or say something, don't sweat it; write them both down and keep going. You can sort it out later when you're doing the editing.

When writing the first draft, you must tell the story to yourself. Get the basic ideas down on paper. Correct the facts later.

Speaking of facts—don't stop writing to look up a date, number, or fact. Write "XX" and keep going. You can make the "XX" red if you want it to stand out so you'll be sure to see it while reading your manuscript. Keep writing and go back later and look up the information. If you stop to look something up, you'll likely lose your momentum. Maybe not, but don't risk it.

Polish your writing and look up facts later. That's called editing. If you try to write a final version (or even a good version) as you go along, most likely, at the end of your writing session, you won't have many words on the page.

Nonfiction writers seldom experience writer's block. Here's why

If you've been around writers much, I'm sure you've heard them talk about "writer's block." It's when they can't think of anything to say. They can't get started putting words on the page. All fiction writers experience this from time to time.

Since you're writing nonfiction, you won't likely experience writer's block. Here's why. Fiction writers have to make up everything they write.

As a nonfiction writer, you're not making up anything. You're telling someone how to do something that you know how to do. If you didn't know how to do what you're writing about, you wouldn't be writing a book about it in the first place.

You'll probably do some research to ensure your facts are correct and up to date, and you may want to do some research to learn what other experts in your field have said about the topic.

But if you were talking to someone and they asked you to tell them how to do something you know how to do, you wouldn't say, "I can't tell you right now because I have writer's block." You could tell them immediately how to do the task being discussed. Later, you could come back and say it slightly differently or in a way that would be easier for the person to understand.

You may decide to explain one part of the process in a little more detail or delete some words if you feel like you rambled too much in one area.

That's what's called editing, when you add, delete, or modify the words you've used to describe how to do something.

You won't have a problem with writer's block if you remember that your job is to write a rough draft.

Points to keep in mind while writing your first draft

- The most crucial point to remember is that your reader wants a transformation—not information. I've said this before, but it's worth repeating. Give this point some serious thought. Can you deliver a transformation?

- Each chapter should stand alone. A lot of readers won't read your book front to back. They'll skip around. They'll start by reading the chapters that interest them most or the ones they think will have the answer to their problem.

- Include personal stories and experiences in your book to keep it from being boring. This also makes you relatable. You want the reader to be able to relate to you. Let them feel that you know their pain and can help them. Your personal experiences should include your successes and your failures. Show that you're human.

- Bring your book alive with stories.

- Include emotions in your book. Your book should not be all facts and academics.

- Don't use a lot of jargon.

- By the end of the book, make sure you've clearly explained your solution to the problem you've promised to solve for the reader and that you've done it in such a way that your reader can implement your solution immediately.

- Don't pad or ramble in your book. A short book is better than one filled with unnecessary words.

Many successful how-to books are short.

The book *Who Moved My Cheese?* was published 25 years ago and is still a bestseller. It has only 108 pages.

Three things that will keep your book on track

Don't lose track of the answers to the following three questions as you write, and your book will stay on track.

1.   Who are your readers? (Retired people, teenagers, housewives, sports fans, etc.—you can't say, "everybody.") Picture one particular person you know who will benefit from what you're writing. Pretend you're talking directly to that person. Doing this will make explaining what you're trying to convey much easier. Think about who needs your information and advice. Who could learn, change, and grow if they had your information?

2.   What are your most important keywords and phrases? (You came up with these back in Chapter 3.) Make sure these keywords and phrases are a prominent part of your book.

3.   What is the title and subtitle of your book? (You came up with a working title and subtitle in Chapter 4.) Review it and be sure you still want to go with that title. As you write your book, make sure it's delivering on what the title and subtitle promised. (You may change your title and subtitle

as you go along—maybe even several times. That's okay. I almost always make slight changes to my subtitle, and sometimes I change my title.)

With these three things nailed down and clearly in your mind as you write, your writing will stay on track and move along quickly. All you have to do is let the words flow.

As Jodi Picoult, the famous author of 37 books, said, *"You can always edit a bad page. You can't edit a blank page."*

Nonfiction books need to have several subheadings in each chapter.

I insert some as I go along, and after I've finished the first draft, I go back and review what I've written, add headings, and almost always move sections around.

Some writers like to create a detailed outline. If you do this, your outline will more or less be your subheadings. I don't do it this way, but you should do what works for you. The most important thing at this point is to cover the topic and get words on the page.

When you have a well-written chapter, you should be able to read the chapter title, scroll through the chapter, read the subheadings, and have a pretty clear idea about what the chapter says.

Reading over the subheadings will also let you know if you have the points in the correct order and if you're describing things in an easy-to-follow way.

I almost always move sections of text around after I write a chapter to get it to flow in a way that will be clear to the reader. You don't want the reader to have to work to understand the points you're trying to get across. You want to provide the information to the readers in a way that's easy for them to comprehend and understand. You don't want your reader to have to think hard about what you're saying.

Include pictures and diagrams

"I don't trust words. I trust pictures." ~ Gilles Peress

This comment describes how a lot of people feel when they're trying to learn something.

Here's an old saying that is so true when explaining things.

"A picture is worth a thousand words."

Many things can be explained better with a picture than by describing them, so consider using some images in your book.

Note: I almost always include several pictures in my books, but I didn't see many places where pictures would help explain things in this book, so I have included only a few images.

A word of caution about pictures

It's crucial how you format pictures in your book. In Chapter 10, I'll explain in detail how to add images and diagrams. Do it wrong, and you could lose money on every book you sell.

You need to compress your photos in eBooks because Amazon charges you a delivery fee for every eBook you sell. The fee is based on the file size of your book. If you have several uncompressed photos, Amazon could be charging you more for each book you sell than you receive for the book.

For printed books, you need to do the opposite. You need to use the highest-resolution version of the pictures you have. A compressed, low-resolution photo in a printed book looks terrible. Amazon doesn't charge you for file size on printed books. They charge you based only on how many pages a book has.

Other miscellaneous comments about writing techniques

Dictating vs. typing?

Some writers use audio-to-text programs so they can talk into a microphone and have the words appear on the page. That way, they don't have to do any typing. If you have trouble writing, try this technique. One of the best programs to do this is *Dragon Naturally Speaking*.

I don't use a speech-to-text program. I find that I'm more productive when I'm typing my manuscript. Use whatever works for you.

Jot down important points and topics as they pop into your head

Sometimes a thought will pop into my head, and I will quickly write it on the page I'm working on (or at the end of the chapter), knowing that that's not where it will end up. I know I'll come across it later and move the words to the place in the book where they should go.

I do that because I don't want to stop and take a chance at losing my train of thought about what I'm writing, and I don't want to forget the profound idea I just had.

This is one of the significant advantages of writing nonfiction. You want to get your thoughts, facts, and opinions down on paper, and then you can arrange them logically in the book.

Grammar and spelling are super important

Having a lot of grammar or spelling errors in your book is a quick way to get several negative reviews. I like to eliminate as many grammar and spelling mistakes as possible before giving my manuscript to my proofreader. The easy way to check your grammar and spelling is to use a program on your computer to do this.

You can have a program on your computer to check grammar and spelling as you go along, check after you finish each chapter, or wait and check after you finish writing your book.

The two most popular grammar-checking programs can be found at Grammarly.com and Ginger.com. They both offer a free version and an advanced paid version.

I use the paid version of Grammarly. It's a Chrome extension. You can download the free or paid version at **Grammarly.com**.

If money is tight, you can use the free version and do just fine. Hopefully, your proofreader will catch any errors your free version misses.

After you've finished writing your book, you may want to consider paying for a one-month subscription to the paid premium version of the Grammarly program and use it to do a more thorough final check of your book.

If you're using MS Word, it does a good job of checking the grammar and spelling of your document, but it's not as thorough as the Grammarly program.

15 final comments about writing your book

1. Speed is not your goal—quality is.

2. Break your writing task into small pieces (that's what your Table of Contents does for you). Your Table of Contents, or TOC, is your outline. Reading the TOC should tell your story and define the flow of how you tell your big idea. If you find that your book is deviating from your outline, change the outline. Don't change the book. I read over my TOC almost every time I'm ready to start writing a new chapter.

3. You need one big idea or unique solution to the problem your book is solving for the reader. It needs to be a big idea that's book-worthy. There's no room in today's market for small ideas. If you have a small idea, save it for a blog post or a chapter in a book.

4. Don't let your book die in the middle. You can have an intriguing Introduction, but your book can die in the middle if you start rambling and don't keep it exciting and moving towards your unique solution. Maybe your solution is a series of steps—that's the way my solution to writing a book is presented in this book.

5. Make sure your book has valuable new information about your topic or technique. You'll find a lot of points and strategies about how to write your manuscript in this book that are different from so-called conventional wisdom. The world is full of people following conventional wisdom about how to write a book, and in most cases, their book never gets finished, or if it does, it's not good and doesn't sell.

6. Set a deadline or goal. Writing so many words per day and setting a date by which to have the first draft completed are reasonable goals. You can also set shorter goals, such as when you will have a draft of your next chapter finished. Note that you don't have to write the chapters in order. I never do. I write the chapters I know the most about and am the most passionate about first, and then I write the next chapter I'm most passionate about. Following this technique, I almost always get near the end of the book and find that I have a chapter or two left that I haven't written about. That's when I accept that the topic is unimportant and doesn't deserve a whole chapter. Sometimes I find that I've already covered the important part of the topic in another chapter or I may omit the topic. Why should I subject my readers to wading through the material if I'm not interested in a topic or don't think it's important?

7. Do your research. Don't draw from only your own experience but also know what other experts in the field think. Maybe you disagree with them, but you still need

to know their thoughts on your topic. Do a lot of research, make notes, watch YouTube videos, and read books and articles. Do some Google searches. You need to know more about your topic than anyone else on the planet. But just because you know all this information doesn't mean you need to include it in your book. It's essential to keep the point in mind that I made earlier—your reader wants a transformation, not information.

Make sure your information is accurate. One of the worst things you can do is state something in your book that's not true. If you do, many of your readers will pick up on it, and then they'll take a lot of the other things you say with a grain of salt.

8. You need a compelling opening line.

9. Reader first. You want your book to be the best, most compelling, emotional experience your reader has ever experienced. The purpose of your book is to answer a question or solve a problem for the reader. They didn't buy your nonfiction book to be entertained. They want a solution to their problem, and your answer will most likely change their lives. Don't let them down. Deliver the solution that your title and subtitle promised.

10. The early part of your book should convince the reader that you understand their problem and are uniquely qualified to solve it. Then, promise them that you're going to deliver a solution. The later part of your

book should deliver on that promise. You can also do this with each chapter because each should stand alone.

11. When you're writing, your only goal is to put words on the page. Do NOT question or critique what you're writing. Not even a little bit. Let the words flow. Some of your best writing will happen when you're letting the words flow. Turn off your internal editor. Always save your editing until at least the next day. Waiting longer is even better.

12. Never stop to look up a fact or number when you're writing. Just insert "XX" and keep writing. You can go back later and look up the information. Don't interrupt your train of thought to look up a fact.

13. Don't let your book die in the middle. The middle of your book is essential. You have a great beginning and can't wait to reach your profound conclusion, but you have to write the middle of the book. Don't fill the middle with marginally interesting points. If you don't fill the center of your book with riveting, eye-opening information, the reader will stop reading and never see your profound conclusion.

One of the primary purposes of each sentence is to compel the reader to read the following sentence and the next chapter. Don't be tempted to fill the middle of your book with mundane information. A dull middle part of the book is the downfall of most unsuccessful books. This is also where many writers lose interest and never finish their books.

The ending of your book will be better and more profound if you do an excellent job of writing the middle. Put a lot of thought and effort into the middle of your book, and don't just muddle through it.

14. You must have a great ending to have a successful book. To have a great ending, give it the time and effort it deserves. By the time you get to the end of your book, you're probably way behind on the schedule you set for yourself and ready to finish the project. You may have several ideas about how you want to conclude your book. There's a saying, "Done trumps everything," and you're ready to be done with your book, but don't rush the ending. I sometimes spend more time writing the end of a book than I do the rest of it.

You'll probably have several ideas about how to end your book. Go with the one that evokes the most emotion. Readers remember what moves them. You want your readers to finish your book thinking, " Holy s # it. I can do this," or "This is the solution to my problem that I've been looking for."

15. Finally, relentlessly edit your book. But first, let it rest for a few days; then, come back to it and start editing. Cut out all the fluff and unnecessary words (and you'll find many of them). Run it through a grammar program (I like Grammarly.com). Edit it until you're happy with every

word. Use a text-to-speech program to read your book back to you. There's a good one included in MS Word. Do this before you turn your book over to a professional proofreader. By hearing the book read back to you, you'll catch many errors you will most likely never notice when you read the manuscript.

If you get this far, you've got it made.

There's still a lot of work to be done after you've finished writing your rough draft, but when you reach this point, you're way further along than many writers ever get.

You've Finished Your First Draft. Now What?

Now you have a terrible first draft. If you don't have a bad first draft at this point, you put too much time and effort into tweaking and working on your draft. If you did that, it means you didn't turn your mind loose and let it go.

As Tom Clancy said in the quote I mentioned previously, "Tell the damn story." The heck with grammar, flow, facts, dates, information, etc.

You've reached a significant milestone when you've written your rough first draft. At this point, you could turn your rough draft over to an editor or ghostwriter and tell them to make a book out of it, but that's not what you want to do.

First, if your first draft is like most of mine, an editor would charge you a fortune to turn it into a good book. And you probably wouldn't recognize it when they got through with it. It wouldn't sound like you.

Now is when you start working on your baby chapter by chapter, but first, give it a few days. Clear your mind and come back to it fresh.

When I do this and start reading what I have written, I sometimes think, *This is good.* Of course, other times, when I'm reading over what I've written, I find myself saying, "This is crap. What nut wrote this?" You'll probably find some chapters that fit into each of the categories I've described.

Forget the old cliché of writing about what you know; instead, write the book you want to read.

One final thing. Click on all of the links in the eBook version to make sure they work. For the printed version, copy and paste each link into the search bar to ensure it works. I recommend doing this again after the book is formatted.

I had a book a few years ago where some links didn't work. A lady gave me a two-star review and said the links didn't work. I immediately fixed the problem and replied to the comment saying that the bad links had been corrected, but almost nobody reads a reply to a comment. That bad review is still showing, and that book never recovered or sold well. Don't let this happen to you.

I don't use as many links now as I used to because I realized that websites change and links stop working. Amazon and readers don't like it when links don't work. Amazon will flag your book as having quality issues when links don't work, and they don't rank a book high when it has quality issues.

The main takeaway from this chapter: I've covered a lot of points in this chapter. Some may be considered common sense, but they're important, so don't dismiss them. I'm sure some of the other points are new to you, and you may be questioning whether they're important or even if they'll work. They're important if you want to write a best-selling book that will make you money.

Chapter 9

You Need a Proofreader—Not an Editor

"There is no more fatal blunderer than he who consumes the greater part of his life getting his living."

~ Henry David Thoreau

If you were writing a novel, you would probably need an editor because when you're writing fiction, you have to keep a lot of balls in the air. Character development, plot, continuity, and other things must work together. This is where an editor can be a big help.

When writing a nonfiction book, you don't have to worry about any of those things. However, you will need a proofreader. No matter how many times you read over your work, you'll never find all the errors. Even professional proofreaders won't catch everything.

That's why it's a good idea to have several people read your book before you publish it. That's one of the many advantages of having a launch team of beta readers, which I'll talk about later.

My undergraduate degree was in electrical engineering, and I worked as a design engineer early in my working life. In engineering school, most of what I was taught was how to design things. After all, that's what engineers do—they design things.

But when I got out of college and started working as an engineer, I spent a lot more time testing designs after I did the design work than I ever spent designing things in the first place.

The same is true with writers—at least, the successful ones spend more time editing and tweaking their manuscripts than they spend writing the first draft.

So don't skip the editing step. After you write a chapter, give it a day (or even longer) and then edit it. Then, wait a few days and edit it again. Do a lot of editing before you turn your work over to your proofreader.

After you finish your book, go back and edit the completed book—even though you've already edited each chapter. By looking at the completed book, I often find that I've said the same thing in different chapters.

I sometimes say the same thing in different chapters because I want each chapter to stand alone. As I have said before, you don't have to read the chapters in order, and a lot of people don't. But sometimes, I find that I've repeated something when I shouldn't have.

Also, in places where you refer to another chapter, such as, "This will be discussed in Chapter XX," be sure to check and make sure that the chapter numbers you're referencing are correct. You'll likely move chapters around and add or delete chapters as you write your book. This will mess up all of your references to chapters.

I usually pay a professional proofreader to read my manuscript, and after they do their work, I have a few friends and other writers read over it. They sometimes find more things that need to be corrected.

I like to have a professional proofreader review the manuscript before I let my friends read it. That way, my friends won't know how bad of a writer I am.

Catch errors by listening to your book being read to you

I've made this point before, but it's worth repeating. One of the best ways to catch problems in your writing is to have the computer read the text back to you using a text-to-speech program. Regardless of how often I've read over a draft, I always find problems when I hear the text read back to me. By all means, don't skip this step in your editing process.

Hearing the text read back to you allows you to catch errors you don't catch when reading it yourself. Your mind fills in missing words and corrects other errors when you read the text, and this is especially true when you read your own material.

MS Word includes a text-to-speech feature. To access it, click "Review" at the top of the page and then "**Read Aloud**."

Hiring an editor is fine if you can afford one. I think an editor is valuable (maybe even essential) if you're writing a novel, but you can save money and get by without one for your nonfiction book. That's what I do.

The main takeaway from this chapter: By all means, hire a good proofreader. Even then, get as many of your friends as you can (and other authors you know) to also read your book. You can never catch all of the errors, but you can work hard to find as many as possible.

Chapter 10

How to Include Photos in Your Book

"A photographer went to a socialite party in New York. As he entered the front door, the host said, 'I love your pictures—they're wonderful; you must have a fantastic camera.' He said nothing until dinner was finished, then: 'That was a wonderful dinner; you must have a terrific stove.'"

~ Sam Haskins

Many things can be explained better with a picture than by describing them with words, so consider using some images in your book.

Here are three important cautions about pictures.

#1. **Don't use pictures you don't own the rights to.** Use pictures you took yourself, pictures you purchased the rights to, or pictures you downloaded from sites that offer copyright-free images. The two websites I use to find royalty-free stock images are Pexels.com and Pixabay.com.

If you want a more extensive selection of pictures and are willing to pay a small fee, you can check out iStock.com. You can purchase the rights to one of their pictures for $12 to $33, depending on the picture. You wouldn't want to buy many pictures at this price, but it might be worth it if you need one great picture for your book cover.

If you need up to ten pictures, you can subscribe to their monthly plan for one month and get ten pictures for $40. I've bought a few pictures from iStock to use on my book covers. They have a large selection of high-quality pictures.

By all means, don't use pictures you downloaded off of the internet from a website or Facebook post. Whether they say so or not, those pictures are copyrighted, and you can get sued for using them.

#2. **Don't use pictures of children if they're recognizable in the picture unless they're your children.** It's against the law in most situations.

#3. **Don't use pictures that are not formatted correctly.** The largest page for any Kindle device is 600 by 800 pixels. If any of your pictures are larger than this, they will screw up the formatting of your eBook.

Also, make sure your pictures are in the .jpg format. Kindle says they'll accept .png and other formats, but they sometimes mess up the pictures when they're not in the .jpg format, so don't take a chance. Make sure all of the pictures in your Kindle book are .jpg.

How you format pictures for eBooks and printed books are different. Do it wrong, and you could lose money on every book you sell. It's essential that you compress photos for eBooks. Here's why.

You need to compress your photos in eBooks because Amazon charges a digital delivery fee based on the file size for each book you sell. If you have several uncompressed photos, Amazon could be charging you more for each book you sell than you receive for the book.

For example, shooting a high-resolution photo with your cell phone or digital camera could easily be five MB or larger. If you were to include five of these 5-MB images in your book, the file size of your book would be 25 MB plus the text file size.

25 MB times 15 cents per MB would mean that Amazon would charge you $3.75 (plus a small amount for the text file size) for each book you sold. If you sold your book for $3.95 and received a 70% commission, you would earn $2.77 per book, but Amazon would charge you $3.75 to deliver your book, so you would lose almost a dollar every time you sold a book.

Using the "Save for web" feature in Photoshop will compress the file size of a picture, and your compressed image will look just as sharp in an eBook as an uncompressed image.

And the file size would only be about 135 KB or 0.135 MB. That would mean for the five compressed 5 MB images in your book, Amazon would only charge you a total of 2¢ (15¢/MB x .135 MB) for all five images in your book.

You can afford to pay Amazon two cents to include the five images in your book, but you can't afford to pay $3.75. The compressed images will look just as sharp, and the human eye cannot tell the difference.

Maybe I should have just told you to compress the images in your eBooks and omit all of these paragraphs explaining why, but I wanted to make sure I got the point across. I didn't want you to put all the work into creating a best-selling book and then lose money on every book you sold.

For printed books, you need high-resolution photos.

You need to use the highest-resolution version of the pictures you have. A compressed, low-resolution photo in a printed book looks terrible. Amazon doesn't charge you a fee based on the file size of printed books. They charge you only based on how many pages a book has.

You can use Adobe Photoshop or the free IrfanView program to resize and compress the images you use in your eBook. The free program GIMP also does an excellent job of resizing images.

Before you compress the image, you'll want to resize it to 600 pixels wide. This will be the right size for your eBook. The program will maintain the correct ratio and automatically calculate the proper height for the picture.

If you want to adjust the size after you insert it into your manuscript, you can grab a corner and resize it.

You'll probably also want to center the image.

Don't try to wrap text around an image in an eBook. It can turn into a disaster. For example, the image doesn't resize when the reader changes the size of the text he's viewing.

Black and white vs. color pictures

A color picture looks better, and photographs in eBooks show up in color, but print books show all pictures in black and white (unless you pay an arm and a leg to have your whole book printed in color).

Having color pictures in children's books and maybe in cookbooks will probably be necessary, but the cost of printing your book in color is not worth it for most nonfiction books. Perhaps, one day, Amazon will allow you to pay to have only two or three pages in color, but you can't do it now.

If you use a color picture in your print book, Amazon will convert it to black and white, but the picture will probably look better if you convert it to a black-and-white image yourself and then adjust the brightness and contrast.

I've done it both ways. It's easier just to put your color picture in the manuscript and let Amazon deal with it.

How to prepare and place images in your book

The process is relatively simple if you're using LibreOffice Writer or MS Word—but only if you know a few secrets.

The first step is to resize the pictures and compress the version of the pictures to be used in the eBook.

Place your cursor where you want your picture to appear. Click on "Insert" in the top toolbar, select "Picture," and then select "This device" to grab a picture from your computer.

Next, right-click on the picture and select "Caption" if you want to add a caption below it. (I think placing a descriptive caption under each picture is a good idea.)

You'll probably want to center the picture and maybe resize it. To resize a picture, click on it, grab the corner, and make it the size you want.

To summarize how to place an image in your book, you should . . .

- Resize the picture (usually to a width of 600 pixels for an eBook and to the width of the text for a printed book).

- Compress the pictures that will be used in an eBook.

- Insert the picture at the desired place in your manuscript.

- Add a caption to the image. To do this, right-click on the image and click "Insert caption."

- Always use the Kindle Book Previewer before publishing your book to ensure the pictures look the way you want them to.

The main takeaway from this chapter: Pictures are an important part of most nonfiction books, so seriously consider including some pictures in your book. But be sure to follow this chapter's directions, comments, and information to prevent your use of pictures from becoming a disaster.

Chapter 11

Formatting Your eBook and Printed Book

"The difference between fiction and reality? Fiction has to make sense."

~ Tom Clancy

If you use a template as you're writing your book, it will be roughly formatted as you go along. That's what I do, but you'll still need to do the final formatting after editing and proofreading.

Size is important, at least it is when it comes to books. For your nonfiction book, make it 6"x 9". This is the most common size for nonfiction books. This is the size I use for all my books.

Fonts

One of the first things you have to do when you start to format your book is select the font you will use. Garamond is one of the most common fonts, and many books use it.

I like to use URW Bookman L. I think it's easier to read. (Note: I didn't use URW Bookman L for this book because it wasn't available in the new formatting software I used.) I set the font size to 12 pt. Novels sometimes go with 11.5 or even down to 11. They do this so the book won't be so large. I like the larger print, so I stick with 12 pt.

To ensure Amazon uses the font you want, embed it in the native program before publishing. Note that you set the font and point size for printed books only. The eBooks are displayed on the buyer's reader according to his set parameters.

Margins

The next thing you need to do when you start formatting your book is to set the margins. I usually set my margins between 0.75" and 1.0" all the way around. You can make the margins narrower or wider. The minimum gutter margin depends on the page count.

Below is a link to Amazon's page that tells you the minimum margins they allow, along with their other publishing and formatting specifications.

aLaptopLife.com/margins

Everyone agrees that the left margin should be justified, but there's some disagreement about the right margin. Some authors like to have it non-justified or ragged. I like to have both the left and the right margins justified. That's the way most books are formatted.

There is not much difference between how you format a print book and an eBook, but a few things are different.

In an eBook, your table of contents and links need to be clickable, and your photos need to be compressed because Amazon charges you a digital delivery fee based on the file size. Compressed photos look the same in an eBook as uncompressed photos.

For the print book, you'll need to add a blank page at the end of some chapters. You'll need to do this so that all new chapters start on a right-hand page. Also, add a blank page at the end of the book. There will be two blank pages because you want to have a page that is blank on the front and back.

For your print books, you don't want to have a heading at the bottom of a page. If it comes out that way, add a blank line and move the heading to the top of the next page.

That's about all the differences, so don't consider publishing a book without making both versions available to readers.

Having both an eBook and a printed version of your book is an essential part of marketing your book. Don't skip this step.

Using a template makes formatting easier

Here's a link to a website where Amazon shows you step-by-step how to use their free downloadable template to format your printed book utilizing MS Word. It also includes a three-minute video.

https://kdp.amazon.com/en_US/help/topic/G201834230

Here is a longer video by Amazon that goes into more detail about how to format your book. This video is 48 minutes long.

https://www.youtube.com/watch?v=kTkMUoxD2TU

In the past, I formatted my books the easy way

I hired someone on Fiverr.com to do the formatting for me. Since I use a template when writing my books, they are somewhat formatted when I send them to the person doing the formatting. There's not much for him to do, so he doesn't charge me much.

I have used a few different people on Fiverr and have been satisfied with them.

As the title of this book says, you can publish your book without spending any money. To do this, format your book yourself. I've done that for some of my books. You will need to take the time to learn a few additional skills. If you've typed your book into a template, that makes it a lot easier. There are several videos on YouTube that show you how to format a book that's typed in MS Word.

The good thing about formatting your book yourself is that you don't have to perfect it the first time. You can use Amazon's Previewer to look at your finished book, and if you see something wrong with it, you can make changes and look at it again.

When selecting a Fiverr designer to do the formatting of your book, look at their feedback rating and comments.

Give them plenty of instructions about how you want your formatting done. Then, use the Amazon Previewer to look at the finished format, and if you see something you want to change, the person doing the formatting will gladly make changes.

I like to have the same person format, both the eBook and the printed book. Describe the work you want them to do, include a copy of your manuscript, and ask the designer for a quote.

When he has a copy of your manuscript, he can see how much work is involved in formatting your book.

Miscellaneous notes about formatting

- **For printed books, submit your manuscript to Amazon as a PDF file**. You'll want to keep a copy of the manuscript in a Word version so you can make changes later if necessary. (I write my books using the Atticus program, and it automatically saves a copy.)

- **For the eBook, submit it to Amazon in the EPUB format**. Even though Amazon says they will accept a Word file for an eBook, don't do it. They've messed up the formatting every time I've tried it.

- Always look at both the eBook and the printed book carefully using the Amazon Previewer to make sure the books are formatted exactly the way you want them.

Last minute update: I formatted this book using the new Atticus.io program. (This is not an affiliate link.) At $147, it was a little more expensive than hiring someone from Fiverr.com to do the formatting, but since I plan on writing a lot more books, I will save money in the long run. I love the program.

The two main things I like about using the program are that it is easy to learn, and anytime I want to change the book, I can make the change myself without having to go back and have someone format it again. Take a look at the program and see if it looks like it will be useful to you.

The only thing I didn't like about it was that it didn't support some of the fonts I like to use, but they're working on adding more fonts. When you own the program, you get all future upgrades at no charge.

The main takeaway from this chapter: You've put a lot of work into writing your book; don't get in a hurry and end up with a crappy book because you didn't format it correctly. Spend the time to learn how to format your book correctly (it's easy), or hire a professional on Fivver.com to format your book for you.

Chapter 12

How to Select the Best Categories

"A blank piece of paper is God's way of telling us how hard it is to be God."

~ Sidney Shelton

In the original version of this book, I went into great detail explaining how to get Amazon to list your book in ten categories. And then, on Tuesday, May 30th, Amazon changed their rules. They announced a totally new way that authors are now required to choose the categories for their books. The old way is gone. You can't use it any longer.

Look on the bright side: Amazon's new way of selecting categories is easier.

With the new rules, instead of jumping through several hoops to select ten categories, you are only allowed to select three.

Amazon skips the trivial steps

You no longer start by telling Amazon the two BISAC categories you think your book should fit into. Instead, you skip that step and tell them which three of Amazon's 17,000 categories you think your book should be listed in. If they agree with you, that's all there is to the process.

Selecting your categories is not as hard as it sounds. Amazon guides you through the process with drop-down menus they provide when you submit your book.

You would like your book to be listed in the categories it would most likely fit in and in categories that don't have much competition. That way, your book could rank #1 in a category even when you were not yet selling many books. For some categories, ranking #1 with only two or three sales a day would be possible.

Before the big change, authors would select some categories with low competition as long as their book was a somewhat reasonable fit, but sometimes they would cross too far over the line and select a category that their book didn't come close to belonging in. If they got too far out of line, Amazon would not approve their selection, or sometimes they would initially approve the selection and then come back later and disallow it. But they were not overly aggressive in policing books being listed in the wrong categories, so a lot of authors were notoriously stepping way over the line.

Authors did this so they could get Amazon to place a coveted badge (like the one shown below) on their book's detail page.

#1 Best Seller in Personal Transformation

The plan was that, hopefully, readers would see the #1 Best Seller badge and not realize that it didn't mean the book was the #1 Best Seller for all books.

Amazon has more than 17,000 categories, so at any given time, there are over 17,000 books that are ranked as the #1 best seller in their category.

Nevertheless, this badge would add credibility to any book and increase sales. I think it could sometimes backfire. For example, if I saw a book about Italian cooking listed as being ranked #1 in the Computers & Technology category, I would know the author was being less than truthful, and I wouldn't buy that book. A lot of other readers probably would feel the same way.

When you're selecting your categories using Amazon's new system, don't just select a broad category, such as "History." Select the main category and then select the subcategory. Then, drill down to a subcategory of the subcategory.

Also, be sure to check the box for "Fiction" or "Nonfiction." Since this book is about marketing nonfiction, I assume your book is nonfiction, so check the Nonfiction box.

Amazon's new rules for choosing categories

Since Amazon has changed their rules about selecting categories, you can have only three categories instead of ten. You select the three categories you want from Amazon's list of 17,000 categories, and then you submit your book. If Amazon doesn't approve all of your three categories, your book is not listed and is placed in what they call "draft mode" until you change your categories and select categories they agree your book belongs in. They are now very strict about this.

You may not be able to find a category that your book will fit in where you can be ranked #1 with only one or two sales a day, but with a little work, you can find categories where it doesn't take many sales a day to be ranked #1.

You can change your category selections, but Amazon recommends not changing categories too often. They say to wait at least a month before you change a category. Changing categories too often will lower your ranking, so put a lot of effort into getting your categories right the first time.

Since you get to choose only three categories, you need to select them carefully. You don't have any to waste as you did in the old days. This could be good news for you if you know how to select your categories because you won't be guessing about categories like most authors will be doing.

If you have books you've previously published using the old system where you have selected up to ten categories, you can go in and delete those ten categories and start over using the new system. That's what Amazon recommends, and I'm going to start doing that for my 27 other books, but first, I want to finish jumping through all the hoops to get this book published.

How to find more categories manually

There are ways you can go in and manually get some of this information about which categories would be the best for your book, but it takes a lot of time.

One way to find categories for your book is to spy on your successful competitors. To find your most successful competitors, search for your most important keywords and see which books Amazon shows you. To see how successful they are, look at the BSR (Best Seller Ranking) and also look to see how many reviews they have.

Here's a free tool that will show you the categories your competitors' books are listed in.

Go to **https://www.bklnk.com** and click the red "Find your Categories" button at the bottom left-hand column. When you click on that link, it will take you to a new page.

You will find a box near the bottom of the second column to enter either the ten-digit ISBN or the ASIN. (Don't enter the 13-digit ISBN.) Enter the number, then click the green **Go Find** box.

Then, at the bottom of the second column (below the **Go Find** box), you'll see all the categories in which the book is listed.

There's a new app that easily gives you all of this information

There is a much easier and faster way to make all of this happen by using an app (also called a program) that will take your keywords and show you a list of categories that your book would fit into, and it will show you how many sales a day it would take to rank #1 and how many to rank #10 in each of those categories. It makes the whole process of selecting categories seem like magic.

The easy way to get this information is to use a feature in the **Publisher Rocket** program. I talked about this program back in Chapter 3 when discussing keywords. For a one-time price of $97, you get lifetime use of the program and all the updates. Dave Chesson is the genius who developed the program and comes out with major updates several times a year. They're all free for life after you own the program.

I've mentioned Publisher Rocket several times in this book, and if it seems like I'm going overboard to convince you to invest in this program, maybe I am, but it's for your own benefit. I'm convinced you can sell more books and make more money the first week (and maybe even the first day) by using this new program than the $97 it will cost you.

Between using the program to find keywords, evaluate your competition, and select categories, it's worth its weight in gold. Not only will knowing the best keywords and categories save you a lot of time trying to find them, but you'll also be way ahead of your competitors, who are trying to guess about this information or spend hours trying to manually dig out the answers.

Go to the link below, scroll down, and click the "See Rocket in Action "box to see what you can do with this program. You'll be amazed at what it will do for you. With this program, you'll have an unfair advantage over your competition. Here's the link:

aLaptopLife.com/rocket

With Publisher Rocket, you can select categories that require only a few sales a day to rank #1. You can also see which categories the books you will be competing with have selected, and you can also see a chart showing the trend of the categories you're considering. Is the category getting more popular, or is it dying?

The main takeaway from this chapter: People don't search for nonfiction books by category as they do fiction books, but selecting the right category will still help you sell more books. That's because if you choose a category (that your book will logically fit into) that doesn't have many competitors, you significantly increase your chances of ranking as the #1 Best Seller in that category.

When your book is ranked as the #1 Best Seller in a category, Amazon places the coveted **#1 Best Seller** orange badge on the book's **detail page**. This banner will add credibility to your book and help boost sales.

Chapter 13

Step-by-Step How to Submit Your Book to Amazon

"The scariest moment is always just before you start. After that, things can only get better."

~ Stephen King

Let's start with how to publish your eBook. In the next section, I'll tell you how to publish your print book. It's slightly different.

Before you start to submit your eBook to Amazon, it's a good idea to create a document with all of the information you're going to need.

- Title

- Subtitle (nonfiction books should always have a subtitle. It allows you to have more keywords and it helps describe and sell the book)

- Author name

- Book description

- Free ISBN or paid ISBN? (If you've purchased an ISBN, have it and the bar code in the file)

- Your two categories (eBooks and print books will be different)

- Seven keywords or keyword phrases

- Price of your book (between $2.99 and $9.99 to get the 70% commission). I've found that the most profitable price for my nonfiction eBooks is $3.99

- **Note:** If you plan to market your book as described in Chapter 16 by starting with a price of 99¢ for the first 48 hours, then you would enter that price here or come back after the book is published and change the price to 99¢.

- Release date (if it's not going to be released immediately)

- Include everything in this document except your book cover and your content file. Have a separate EPUB file of your content for your eBook and the PDF version for your print book. Also, have a different file for your book covers. These files should be stored where they're easy to find.

Go to the Kindle Direct Publishing website at **kdp.amazon.com** and click on the **Sign-in** button if you already have an account, or click on the Sign-up button if you don't.

Note: KDP stands for Kindle Direct Publishing. You'll see it written both ways.

Before Amazon publishes your book, you'll need to furnish them with your banking information and tax information (Social Security number or your business tax ID number).

After your account is set up and you have logged in, click on the **Bookshelf** button and the yellow **Create** button. Then click on the **Kindle eBook** box below the words **Create a New Titl**e.

The rest of the process is simply filling in the boxes. Most of them are straightforward. Here are a few comments for some of the boxes that might be confusing.

Note: Copy and paste the book description that you've already written back in Chapter 7. If you haven't already formatted your description, look at the directions in Chapter 7 and format it. You want it to stand out and be easy to read. By all means, don't just have one long paragraph. Make headings larger, put some text in bold, and use bullet points to make the text easier to read and understand.

Next, enter the keywords you came up with in Chapter 3. Don't repeat any keywords that are used in your title or subtitle. It won't hurt anything, but repeating a keyword doesn't help as it used to do with Google. It's just a waste of one of your keyword boxes.

Next is the Categories section. Use the pull-down menu to select your three categories. Drill all the way down, and don't select broad categories. You would like to select categories that the book fits in that don't have a lot of competition. That way, it's easier to be ranked as #1 in a category.

If you need help selecting your best categories, use the Publisher Rocket program discussed back in Chapter 3.

Since your book is not a children's book, you'll leave the section blank about the age range.

When you finish filling in everything on the first page, click the yellow **Save and Continue** button at the bottom. This will take you to the next page, which starts by discussing **Digital Rights Management (DRM)**.

I always select "No" for Digital Rights Management (DRM) in the Manuscript box. If you want to know more about this, you can click on the phrase **"How is my Kindle eBook affected by DRM?"** and you'll see an explanation. You can't change this setting after you publish your book.

The next step is to upload your manuscript.

Upload your manuscript in an EPUB file format—NOT a .doc or .docx file. Amazon will accept a .doc and a .docx file, but they will likely make a mess of your book formatting if you don't send the manuscript to them in an EPUB file. As of June 28, 2021, Amazon stopped accepting the Mobi format.

When uploading a print book, you'll submit it as a PDF. We'll talk about that later

If you need to know how to convert your .doc or .docx file into an EPUB file, just Google it. If you're having someone format your eBook, tell them to send you the finished results as an EPUB and a .docx file.

Next, you'll upload your book cover. I assume you already have your cover designed, as was discussed in Chapter 5. Don't be tempted to click on the yellow **Launch Cover Creator** button. You'll end up with an ugly cover, in my opinion. Follow the steps in Chapter 5 to come up with a killer cover design.

Click on the circle to select **Upload a cover you already have**. It has to be in either a PDF or TIFF format.

Next, click **Launch Previewer**. Amazon will take a little time to convert the files, so be patient. When it finishes processing the files, take the time to carefully look through your whole book to make sure everything is correct and your book looks the way you want it to look.

In the next box, you enter an ISBN, but this is not required for an eBook, so leave this blank.

Then click on the yellow **Save and Continue** button and move on to the final page of the submission process.

Check the box that says, **"Enroll my book in KDP Select."** If you want to know more about the advantages of enrolling your book in the KDP Select program, you can read all about it on Amazon. You can change your selection later, but for now, take my word for it and just do it.

Then, for territories, select **All territories**, and for Primary Marketplace, select **Amazon.com** if you're in the US.

Next, click on the **70%** circle and set your price. To get the 70% commission, you have to price your book between $2.99 and $9.99. I've run tests, and I've found that I get the same number of sales at $3.99 for my nonfiction books as I do at $2.99. I have friends selling fiction books, and they say they sell a lot more books at $2.99. I go with the default pricing for all of the other countries.

I think these prices make sense because if someone has a problem and wants to know how to do something, whether the book is priced at $2.99 or $3.99 will probably not make a difference in whether they buy your book.

But if they're looking for a book to read for entertainment, they probably read a lot of books, and there are plenty of books to choose from in the $2.99 range, so why select a book at $3.99? These comments are my opinions and observations based on limited testing.

Bottom line: Price your nonfiction eBook at $3.99 after all of your promotions. You can experiment with a higher or lower price later, but with my testing, I've found $3.99 to be the most profitable price point.

Note: If you're going to be promoting your book by starting your eBook price at 99¢ for two days, as will be discussed in Chapter 16, then select a 35% royalty instead of 70%. You're only offering this price for two days. Then you'll take it up to $2.99 for a month and then to your final price of $3.99. It's easy to change your price anytime you want to.

The Book Lending option is automatically selected when you select the 70% commission option, so there's nothing for you to do in this box.

At the bottom of the page, I usually click the circle saying, **"I am ready to publish my book now."** I don't do pre-orders. I think that's useful only for well-known authors.

One significant disadvantage of selecting the pre-order option is that if you choose it and don't get many orders (and you may not since you haven't started promoting your book yet), Amazon will decide that your book is not going to sell well and they won't rank it high. You can do pre-orders only on eBooks—not printed books.

One advantage of doing pre-orders is that all of the pre-orders will count as orders on the day the book goes live, so it could give you a big sales day if you have a lot of pre-orders.

Finally, you will click the yellow **Publish Your Kindle eBook** button, and you're finished with the eBook submission.

A note at the bottom of the page says it could take up to 72 hours for your title to be available for purchase on Amazon, but my experience is that the book will be available in less than 24 hours.

How to publish the printed version of your book

It's almost like the process of submitting an eBook, but there are a few things that are different.

You'll need your manuscript formatted for print. A few things about the formatting that will be different will be that the margins may be different for the inside and outside edges of the pages to allow for the binding.

Also, your cover will be different. You'll need a front cover for an eBook, but for a printed book, your cover will need to include a back cover and a spine. All three components will be in one file.

You can't finish designing your cover until you have your print book formatted and know how many pages will be in the book. You need this information to know how wide to make the spine and how to set the margins.

You have to select whether you want your cover to be matt or glossy. I always go with glossy. I think it looks better and more professional. And I go with white paper. Whether you go with white or cream paper slightly affects the book's thickness.

You have to have an ISBN to sell your book on Amazon. If you haven't purchased a number and don't want to spend the money, click on the box that says, **"Assign me a free KDP ISBN."** Doing this means you can't sell your book anywhere except on Amazon, but that's where most books are sold.

I have purchased a block of ISBNs and always supply my own. This gives me the freedom to sell my books elsewhere besides Amazon, but I've never sold any of my books at other outlets.

For your first book, I recommend saving money and letting Amazon provide you with a free ISBN. If you have some money in your budget to invest in your book project, use it for a proofreader or cover designer.

You have to select the size of your book. I suggest you go with a 6″ by 9″ for your nonfiction book. A lot of authors publishing novels go with a 5″ x 8″ book, but I always go with the 6″ x 9″ size for my books.

Select "No bleed" white paper instead of cream and glossy for the cover instead of matt. That's the way I do it.

I price my print books at $12.95 or $13.95.

Start with this price (unless your book is over 250 pages). You can adjust it later and see how it affects your sales and profit. I like to set my price at a point where I make about $5.00 per book.

That covers all of the things that are different about publishing a print book instead of an eBook.

After you've published both the eBook and the print version, you're ready to start promoting your books and getting reviews. I'll cover that in the following three chapters.

Congratulations. You have published your eBook and printed book on Amazon. If you haven't published your book yet, at least you know how, and you won't have any problem when you get to this part.

The main takeaway from this chapter: There are a lot of steps involved in the publishing process, but they're all easy. Amazon walks you through every step. Follow the information provided in this chapter, and you won't have any trouble.

Chapter 14

How to Create and Use a Launch Team

"You can be young without money, but you can't be old without it."

~ Tennessee Williams

Most authors publish their books on Amazon and sit back and wait for orders to come in. Most of them are surprised when nothing happens.

They're leaving out one of the most critical steps in the book-selling process. They don't have a book launch team.

Having a book launch team is essential to kick off your book-selling process. I know. I've launched books without a book launch team. The books I released with a book launch team are still selling well, and some of the ones I launched without a book launch team never got off the ground.

What is a "book launch team"?

It's a group of people you recruit to help you market your book in the first few days after the book is released.

The primary purpose of a book launch team is to get a lot of people to post reviews all at once as soon as your book is published.

They can help create excitement and buzz about your book by posting comments and announcements on their members' Facebook groups, sending messages to the people on their email lists, and posting reviews on Amazon.

They don't have to buy the book from Amazon to post a review on Amazon, but if several of them do buy the book, that would be a big help. It will help your rankings, and reviews from people who have purchased your book will show up as being from a "Verified Purchase."

Even though a person doesn't have to buy your book to leave a review, they must have spent at least $50 on Amazon.com during the last 12 months. Amazon will accept reviews only from active Amazon customers.

My secret way to create a launch team

If you start asking people to be on your launch team, you probably won't get a lot of takers. Agreeing to be on a team of any kind usually means it will take up a significant amount of your time. If someone asked me to be on a team, I would probably come up with several reasons why I wouldn't have the time to do it.

If you ask people to be on your launch team, you might end up with only two or three of your closest friends, and even they might not put much effort into it. There's an easier and better way to put together a launch team and end up with several people on it.

The secret to success is that you don't call it a team.

To put together your launch team, ask people to be one of your Beta Readers.

As a beta reader, they will feel like they're on the inside. They'll get a copy of your new book before anyone else—even before it's published.

They don't even have to read all of it. You just want them to look at a few chapters and give you their opinion. Everybody likes to give opinions.

It's simple. Ask people to be one of your beta readers instead of asking them to be on your launch team, and you'll find a lot more people will agree to do it.

You do it all by email. In the next chapter, I'll show you how to make it happen step by step, and I have included the emails I use to recruit my beta readers.

The process is simple and easy. And best of all, it works like magic. Follow the steps outlined in the next chapter, and you will quickly have 25, 50, or even 100 people on your launch team- but be careful not to call them your launch team.

As I said, most people don't want to commit to being on a team. The fact that they're your launch team is your secret.

I don't want to waste your time by describing how to make all of this happen in this chapter and then again in the next chapter about getting reviews, so I'll wait and explain the process in detail in the next chapter. After all, getting reviews and putting together a launch team are part of the same process.

The main takeaway from this chapter: It's essential to have a launch team to help you promote your book when it's first published, but asking people to take the time to be on a team won't get you many takers. You must be a little creative in how you go about it.

Chapter 15

My Five Easy Ways to get Reviews

"We are all broken. That's how the light gets in."

~ Ernest Hemingway

The most important thing you can do to have a successful and profitable book is to get reviews. And you need to keep getting reviews because Amazon gives more value to recent reviews than they do to older ones.

There are a lot of techniques you can use to get reviews. Getting reviews follows the 80-20 rule, like most everything else. This means that if you used every known technique to get reviews, you would find that you got 80% of your reviews from only 20% of the things you did. So why not only do that 20% of review-grabbing techniques and forget about the rest?

In this chapter, I'll reveal the 20% of review-gathering techniques that I've found that give me 80% of my reviews. You can do all of the methods I describe without spending any money.

Who can leave a review on Amazon?

Amazon keeps changing the rules, but basically, the person doing the review can't be a relative or close friend. (It's interesting that relatives and close friends are encouraged to leave reviews for audiobooks.)

Having the same last name doesn't automatically classify someone as a relative, but living in the same household or having the same billing address on their credit card does.

People can leave a review whether they've purchased your book or not. The only requirement is that they have spent at least $50 buying things from Amazon within the last 12 months and that they're not a close friend or relative.

How to keep Amazon from deleting your reviews

You have to work hard to get reviews, so you don't want Amazon to delete any of them. Follow the rules and advice below to keep from having any of your hard-earned reviews deleted.

- If someone writes a review and has the same address as you, Amazon will assume they are related to you and delete it.

- If a reviewer has the same last name as you, Amazon won't delete the review, but a reader might view it with a grain of salt.

- If two reviews come from people with the same payment method (credit card, bank account, etc.), Amazon will delete one of them and maybe even both of them. Here's something else to consider. If you let a friend use your credit card to buy something a year ago, and then that friend posted a review of your book, Amazon would likely consider that review fraudulent and delete it.

- Amazon knows most of the companies selling reviews, and if you have reviews from any of these companies, Amazon will delete them, so don't pay for reviews.

- Amazon hasn't stated this yet, but if someone buys your book and then immediately leaves a review, Amazon knows they couldn't possibly have read the book. Also, if it's an eBook, Amazon knows how many pages a reader has read. It would be better if a reader could wait a day or two after receiving a print book to leave a review. And if it's an eBook, if they would thumb through the book fast, I think Amazon would consider that the book has been read. (Amazon doesn't know how fast someone can read, but they know whether they've seen the pages or not.) If someone has read more than 10% of an eBook, Amazon now says they can't return it for a refund. You might be surprised by all that Amazon knows about their customers.

- Don't search for your book, and when you find it, copy the link and send it to someone (or even worse, several people) and ask them to go to the link and leave you a review. There's a lot of coded information in that link, and Amazon can tell what is happening. It's a lot better to tell the person to go to Amazon, search for the title of your book or a keyword phrase, find your book, and then leave their review. That helps your book rank high for the phrase that was searched for.

- Amazon's rules say that when you give someone a free copy of your book (either a physical copy or a PDF) to review, the reviewer should state in their review that they received a free copy for review. Whether they say it or not, it's not your concern. It's not something you can control. Your job is to tell them that when you send them the free eBook.

- If you think one or more of your reviews have been

deleted when they shouldn't, you can contact Amazon and explain why you believe the review should not have been deleted. They will do a manual review, and if they find that there is nothing fishy going on, they'll reinstate the link.

Reviews are super critical to having a successful book

One recent study showed that 33% of readers look at reviews before deciding whether to buy a book or not. That's one of the reasons you need to have a flood of reviews posted on the day your book is released.

You need to start the process of getting reviews before your book is published.

Here are my five techniques for getting book reviews

#1. Send PDF copies to beta readers before publication (Note that this technique has a few follow-up steps, but I'm lumping them all together and treating them as one technique.)

Beta Readers is another name for your launch team.

A beta reader is someone who reads your book (or part of it) before it's published. Usually, you want a few beta readers to act like proofreaders and help you find errors in your book, but in this case, you're using beta readers to get early reviews.

Early reviews are essential. Here's how to get those early reviews.

Set up a spreadsheet with the names and email addresses of as many people as you can think of to be your beta readers—25, 50, 100, or more. Then, add to the list as more names come to mind. Two weeks before the scheduled release date of your book, send each of them a personal email. Since you're sending a personal email, you can personalize each email to fit the recipient.

Here's the subject line for the email.

[Their first name], I need your help

Here's the body of the email.

Hi [Their first name],

(If you know the person personally, add a one-line comment, such as, "I enjoyed talking with you the other day." Or, "I hope you enjoyed your trip."

I'm writing because I've been working on my book, shown below. I've attached a prepublication PDF copy for you.

(Include an image of your book cover here, followed by the title and subtitle as shown below.)

How to Write a Nonfiction Book and Publish It on Amazon

A Complete Step-By-Step Beginner's Guide to

Writing and Publishing Your First Book—at Zero Cost

It will be going live on Amazon on (enter a date that's a week or two away).

Getting a lot of reviews when the book is first released is one of the most important things an author can do to help make a new book successful.

That's what I'm trying to do, and I'd love your help with this.

What I'm asking you to do is to skim through the PDF copy of the book I've attached, read a few chapters in the next week, and post an honest customer review on Amazon the day the book is published (or within a day or two after it goes live). It will be going live on Amazon on (include the date again when the book will be live on Amazon).

Your review doesn't have to be a detailed book review. It can be a one or two-sentence comment about something in one chapter you liked or found interesting.

*Let me know what you think, and, of course, **if you find any typos or errors in the book**, I would appreciate it if you would let me know. I'm sure my proofreader didn't catch everything.*

Thank you so much, [their first name].

[Your name]

***P.S.** Who knows, after reading parts of the book, you might decide you're ready to write your own book.*

(**Note:** In the P.S., add a benefit the reader will get from reading part of your book; what I included above is just an example for my book.)

The day before the launch, send everyone on your list another email saying something like this:

This is just a reminder to let you know that my book will be live on Amazon tomorrow, so please don't forget to post your review. I also wanted to let you know that the eBook will be on sale for 99¢ for the first 48 hours.

*If you have time to buy a copy before you post your review, that would help a lot. **Reviews based on a Verified purchase are much more valuable in Amazon's eyes.** But if you don't have time, don't worry. Just post your review. The number of reviews is what's really important.*

***How to post your review.** To post your review, go to Amazon, and in the "Books" department, search for "**How to Write a Nonfiction Book**" or some other phrase that's* *in the title or subtitle. Click on my green book image and scroll down to near the bottom of the page, where you'll see the heading "**Customer Reviews**." Below that, you'll see the heading "**Review this product**," and below that will be a box that says "**Write a customer review**." Click on that box and post your review. That's all there is to it.*

Thank you so much (their first name) for helping me kick off the launch of my book.

Take care,

(Your name)

After the launch

When you give a free book to people (even your friends), don't expect many of them to post a review. It's just a fact that everyone is busy, and only a few people will get around to posting a review for you. If you expect it to be this way, you won't be disappointed. Your job is to get busy and continue promoting your book.

#2. Get active on social media

Even before you start writing your book, join several groups on social media that are on the general topic of your book. Start reading the comments and replies. See what people are interested in and what their thoughts, fears, problems, and ideas are. This will help you understand your target audience.

But don't just read the posts, be a contributor. Answer questions and post your comments, but don't be controversial.

In addition to learning a lot about your market, you can post information about your book and the release when you're ready to start promoting it. Your new book will be much more warmly received when you're known in the group.

Many moderators don't like to see someone promoting a book without being an active member of the group. Your goal should be to become active in the groups you'll use to announce and promote your book. You don't have to be super active, but read all the posts and become moderately active.

Join social media groups on Facebook, Twitter, Instagram, LinkedIn, TikTok, or whatever. Which media groups you should join depends on your target audience.

For example, if your target audience is mainly older people, TikTok wouldn't be a good channel to reach them. I mostly use Facebook. I've had excellent responses promoting my books through Facebook groups.

I have author friends who have had a good response on Instagram. But unless you already have a large following on the other social media platforms, they may not be worth your time. You only have so much time. Make sure you spend your time doing the things that are the most productive.

Make a post on your social media groups when you release your book and state that it's available for only 99¢ for the next 48 hours. A few weeks later, when you offer the book for free for 48 hours, you should announce that on all of your Facebook or other social media accounts.

You should also announce when the discount price will be going away, such as saying, "Today is the last day my book will be available for 99¢. Tomorrow, the price will go back up to the regular $3.99 price."

#3. Editorial reviews

These are valuable reviews that many authors fail to get. These reviews carry more clout and are usually more persuasive than customer reviews. They're reviews from other authors, publications, etc. You typically have to ask for these reviews. You can send them a PDF copy of your book before it's published and ask them for a review that you can post in the **Editorial Review** section of Amazon's listing.

You can add **Editorial Reviews** at any time, so long after you've published your book when you meet another author or anyone whose opinion you think will add credibility to your book, ask them to give you a review that you can include in your **Editorial Review** section on your book's Amazon Detail page. Remind them they can include a reference to their book, blog, YouTube channel, or whatever in their by-line. You can have four Editorial Reviews for your printed book but only one for your eBook.

#4. Get reviews by making your eBook free for two days

Amazon lets you set the price of your eBook to zero for five days, once every 90 days. I recommend setting your price to zero for two days and letting the whole world know about it. You probably won't be able to let the whole world know that your book is free, but you can let a large percentage of the people who buy books in your niche know it. Here's how to do it.

First, post on all of the groups on social media that you're a member of, telling them that your book is free for the next 48 hours. Also, send an email to everyone on your email list.

Here's another way to tell the world that your book is free. Dozens of websites post a list to their subscribers every day, giving them a list of all the books that are free that day. You can submit your book to the sites, and they will include it on their list when your book is free.

You have to follow their rules. Some of them want you to have at least five reviews, and they want you to let them know a week or so ahead. It's free to get the sites to include your book in their list, but some of them try to get you to pay them a small fee to be featured or be at the top of their list. Maybe this is worth it. I don't know. I've never paid to have my book featured.

You can submit the information to one website at a time (there are dozens of websites), telling them your book will be free. This is time-consuming, but it's free.

The way I do it is I spend $29 to use the tool that will submit my book to 25 of the most important sites that send out information about free book listings. Below is a link to the tool I use. I submit the information to them, and they do all the heavy lifting. Here's the link. This is not an affiliate link.

https://bookmarketingtools.com/submission-tool-featur es

Use this link-gathering technique about a month after you've launched your book when you have at least five or ten reviews. You will get several reviews when you use this technique, and you'll also sell some books.

There are two reasons you'll sell some books when you use this technique. Some people will go to Amazon to get the free book and find out they're too late. The two free days have already passed. Then, some of them will go ahead and buy the book.

The other reason you'll sell a few books is that some readers will want the book's printed version, so they'll buy it. But they wouldn't have known about your book if you had not announced that it was free and gotten all of the publicity. I use this every time I publish a book, and I make way more than the $29 I spend to use the tool described above.

The last time I used this technique, I gave away approximately 2,500 books and received 25 reviews. Many books never receive 25 reviews. Most of the people who received the free book were never going to buy the book anyway. I would say that most of the people who downloaded the free book didn't even read it.

Spending $29 to get 25 reviews is a good deal, as far as I'm concerned. I'll gladly pay a little over a dollar each to get reviews.

Of course, it's against Amazon's rules to pay someone to give you a review, and they will ban you if they catch you paying for links, but the technique of giving away free books and asking for an honest review is encouraged by Amazon. That's why they have the feature built into their marketing techniques that lets you set your price to zero for five days every 90 days.

Another good thing about this technique is that Amazon counts it as a sale when someone "buys" your eBook for "zero" dollars. And when they leave a review, it's listed as a review from a *Verified Purchase*.

#5. Ask for reviews at the end of your book

This is so simple, but a lot of authors forget to do this. How many books have you read where the author didn't ask you to leave a review when you got to the end of the book?

Doing this is simple. At the end of your book, add a statement asking for reviews. Say something such as this.

*If you enjoyed this book, please leave a review on Amazon. **I read every review,** and they help new readers discover my book.*

I've found that pointing out that you read all of the reviews helps you get more of them. Who wants to write a review if no one will ever read it? Reading your reviews will help you learn what people like and dislike about your writing style. Knowing this will help you when you're writing books in the future.

You can also go back and make corrections if someone points out errors or omissions. You can change the text of your print book and eBook anytime.

If you've already published your book and didn't ask for a review at the end, it's easy to go back and add this statement. As I've said many times in this book, you can't change the title or subtitle, but Amazon allows you to change the content. Make the change and re-upload your manuscript.

One last point about reviews

For your book to sell well over a long period of time, you must continue to get reviews. It would be nice if you could work hard, get several reviews, and then forget about getting reviews and work on your next book, but it doesn't work that way.

The more books you sell, the more organic reviews your book will get, but you also need to keep poking the process and repeating some of the steps above to help keep new reviews coming in.

For example, you can offer your book free for two or three days now (and, of course, post that it's free on social media). And you should also constantly be thinking of people you can send a PDF copy to and ask them to post a review for you.

Remember, Amazon values recent reviews way more than old ones when it comes to ranking.

The main takeaway from this chapter: One of the most important things you can do to have a successful and profitable book is to get a lot of reviews. The techniques in this chapter show you how to get those reviews the easy way, but you still have to take action and do the work.

Chapter 16

Marketing Your Book

"My aim is to put down on paper what I see and what I feel in the best and simplest possible way."

~ Ernest Hemingway

You've put blood, sweat, and tears into writing your book. Now, it's time to put your heart and soul into marketing it. One of the worst things you can do is publish your book, sit back, and wait to see what happens.

How do you find readers for your book? You don't.

Authors don't find readers. Readers find books.

Think about the last book you bought. What convinced you to purchase that book? Did the author send you an email asking you to buy it? Did you see an ad for the book somewhere? Probably neither of these things caused you to buy the last book you purchased.

More than likely, you bought the book for one of two reasons. A friend recommended it, or you searched for a keyword or phrase on Amazon about a topic you were interested in and found the book. It's simple.

You found the book. The author didn't find you.

That's all there is to marketing a book. Your book has to either be found on Amazon when someone is searching for a topic or someone has to recommend it.

The person recommending your book doesn't have to be a close personal friend of the reader. It can be a mover and shaker in the industry that the reader follows on the internet and trusts.

Introduction to book marketing

Let's get down to the nitty-gritty of how to market your book. There are hundreds of techniques and ways to market your book, but you don't have the time to try all of them. Some of them can take a lot of time, work, or money.

In this chapter, I will cover the few proven techniques I've used to sell thousands and thousands of books with zero money spent on advertising.

Contrary to what most writers think, writing and publishing your book is only half your job. You should put as much effort into marketing your book as you put into writing it.

Most authors put almost zero effort into marketing their books. That's great news for you. If they did put as much effort into marketing as they did into complaining about why their books were not selling, they would be selling a lot more books.

I'm guilty of not putting as much effort into marketing a book as I should at times. Most of the time, after I write a book, I would rather get busy and start writing on my next book instead of doing everything I can to promote and market the book I have just published. You can't do that and expect to have a successful book.

Amazon gives a slight priority in ranking new books for about a month, and if your book starts to sell well during that time, they'll continue promoting it for another 60 days. So, it's important for you to hit the ground running when you launch your book.

Don't publish your book and wait to see how it sells, and if it's not selling well within a month or so, then think about doing some marketing. If you do this, you've missed most of the opportunity to have Amazon promote your book for you.

That's why after you've done everything described in this book about selecting the right keywords and categories, creating your title, subtitle, book cover, etc., to have a successful and profitable book, your job is simple (at least simple to describe). You need to get reviews, publicity, and sales as soon as your book is published.

When a book starts selling, it will start getting organic reviews, and momentum will keep it selling. I have books I wrote seven years ago that are still selling well.

One of the many advantages of writing books is doing the work once and getting paid monthly for years.

Doing the work one time consists of more than just writing the book. You also have to do a serious job of marketing it, and most of that work should be done when you first launch your book.

There are dozens of ways to market your book, and there are a ton of videos, books, blogs, etc., with gurus telling you how to do it. I'm sure most of the techniques they describe work to an extent, but some require a lot of time or money.

I've boiled book marketing down to the seven techniques I've found that works the best for me when marketing a book. And none of them cost any money.

Here are my Seven Best Book Marketing Techniques

#1. Amazon will sell your book for you, but you have to do your part

The easiest way to sell your book is to let Amazon sell it for you—and they will if you follow the steps I've outlined.

Do the six things below, and Amazon will sell your book for you

1. Write a quality book about a topic people are interested in.

2. Use profitable keywords in your title, subtitle, and seven keyword slots.

3. Write an intriguing title and a captivating subtitle.

4. Create a killer book cover.

5. Write a compelling book description.

6. Get a ton of reviews—then get a few more.

How to do all of these things is covered in previous chapters. Make sure you do each of these things before you expect Amazon to market and promote your book.

To get Amazon to sell your book, you need to do a great job of each of the above tasks. It sounds simple, and it can be, but if you do a poor job on even one of these six things, Amazon won't promote your book very well.

Amazon promotes winners. If your book sells well, Amazon will promote it for free to increase sales. To take advantage of this process, you must promote your book aggressively when it is first released. Early sales are extremely important.

#2. Rank on the first page or die

It's a cold, hard fact that if your book doesn't appear on Amazon's first page when someone searches for your important keyword phrases, your book will die.

A recent study showed that books on the first page got 80% of all the clicks when someone searched for a keyword or phrase. And the first three books on page one got over half of those clicks.

Only 30% of shoppers even look past page one of the search results. If you want Amazon to sell your book for you, you have to get ranked on the first page (top 20 books) of the search results for the keywords and phrases your potential readers will be searching for.

Then, after you get your book on Amazon's first page (meaning ranked in the top 20 books for some of your important keywords), your next job is to get ranked in one of the top five positions (about half of the people who buy a book online buy one of the books that show up in one of the top five search results). Then, as your sales continue and you get more reviews, hopefully, your book will show up in the coveted #1 slot for one or more keywords.

When you achieve these levels of success, Amazon will start marketing your book for you. They'll even send emails recommending your book to buyers they think will be interested in it. (And with Amazon's vast database, they know who would likely be interested in your book.)

People trust Amazon's recommendations. You won't see much response if you send an email to someone you don't know asking them to buy your book, but if they receive an email from Amazon recommending your book, they will likely stop and look at it and maybe buy it.

Amazon has the largest database in the world of book buyers. They know every book that a buyer has ever bought from them. They know who would likely buy your book if they knew about it, so Amazon makes sure these book-buyers know about your book—if they determine it would be profitable for them to promote it. That's why getting early sales is so important.

#3. How to use your beta readers to help sell your book

The primary purpose of your beta readers is to get a lot of reviews when your book is first published. But you can also use them to boost sales. Your beta readers are your launch team. Ask them to post comments about your book on their social media platforms and in their blogs, newsletters, and podcasts. And if they have a YouTube channel, ask them to comment about the book in one of their videos if the topic fits. Also, ask them to recommend the book to their friends.

These steps will result in some extra book sales and keep the buzz alive, which will result in even more book sales. You'll get more organic reviews as you sell more books, which will help your book sales.

#4. Use price to market your book

When you release your book, price it at 99¢ for 48 hours. Since Amazon says it can take up to 72 hours after you push the "Publish" button before your book is live and available for purchase (it usually takes less than 24 hours), wait until your book is actually available before you start counting towards the 48 hours.

Announce this special price everywhere, saying that it's for 48 hours only. Then raise your price to $2.99. Getting a lot of sales soon after it's published will help your book to rank high on Amazon. And, of course, ranking high will help your sales.

Some authors like to price their book at 99¢ for a week, but I like to do it for only 48 hours. This makes buying your book more urgent. Either way is acceptable.

After 48 hours, change the price to $2.99. After two weeks, increase the price to $3.99, but each time you raise the price, announce on social media and to your email list that the price is going up tomorrow. The $3.99 price is where you'll leave the price except for special promotions.

Announcing that the price is going up and that the lower price will no longer be available is what's called, in marketing terms, the takeaway. It's been proven to work time after time.

When making social media posts, it's good to only post when you have "News of value." In other words, post when you have something important to say, and the end of a low price is for sure news of value.

You don't want to post a comment on Facebook and say, "Oh, by the way, my book is still available. Go buy it." That's the purpose of your post, but you have to word it differently and make it sound like it's news. It is news if the price is about to change.

After about a month, offer your eBook for free for two days. When you enroll your book in the Amazon kdp program (which I recommend you do), they allow you to offer your book for free for five days every 90 days.

When people "buy" your book for zero dollars, you don't make any money, but Amazon counts it as a sale. When someone gets the free book and then leaves a review, it's listed as a review from a "Verified Purchase," which carries more weight for both Amazon and potential buyers.

How to use this technique is described in detail in the previous chapter about getting reviews. But in addition to getting reviews, this technique will give you a brief bump in sales because a lot of people will be exposed to your book, and some will decide they want to buy the paperback version instead of getting the free eBook. Also, a lot of people will see the information about the book being free, and by the time they get around to checking it out, the book will no longer be free, and many of them will go ahead and purchase it.

#5. Using social media to market your book

When you're posting about your book on social media, remember that "facts tell and stories sell." What is the purpose of your book? What is the story behind your book? Why did you write the book? People who feel like they know you are more likely to buy your book.

As soon as your book is launched, announce it on social media (with a picture). Then, post updates every few days, such as the book now has 20 reviews, it's ranked #1 in New Releases, or it's #3 in the XYZ category—anything that's even remotely newsworthy.

Post this information on your Facebook page and any Facebook groups you're a member of. Of course, post it only on the Facebook groups interested in the topic of your book, and be sure to follow the group's rules. This is important.

Also, post it on all other social media platforms you're a member of and ask your beta readers to post it to their groups. When someone says something good about your book, that's more believable than when you say something about your book.

If you have a lot of reviews, you can say something like, "The book already has 50 five-star reviews, and it's only been available for two weeks."

Continue building buzz and anticipation about your book on social media

You need to market yourself as well as your book. Having a presence on social media is important. Readers are more likely to buy your book if they feel they know you. If you have a newsletter, a podcast channel, you're a blogger, or you have a YouTube channel, make the most of it. Do all of this to keep the buzz alive.

To get some pre-launch buzz, you can mention in your newsletter or any other channels that you have a book coming out soon. Maybe ask your audience which of two different book covers they like better or which title they like better—anything to build the buzz and anticipation.

#6. The Secret A+ Content Marketing Technique

A+ Content is Amazon's new, free secret tool that will boost your sales. Not many writers are using this technique, making it even more profitable for you.

There's one catch. You can't use A+ Content unless you have a registered trademark for your brand. I'm going into a lot of the details here because there's buzz that Amazon may soon let all authors use A+ Content, and I want you to be prepared when it happens. So, let's continue.

A+ Content is a new feature that allows Amazon users to submit up to five additional pictures and pieces of text to provide more compelling reasons to buy a book. After you submit your information, Amazon will place your A+ Content on your product detail page above the Editorial Reviews.

Amazon allows you to use up to five modules in your A+ Content, and both books used all five. A module is what Amazon calls a picture, graphic image, or banner.

Only a few books are taking advantage of this new feature.

In the box below, you can click on the A+ Content Examples link and see several more examples of how books use this new marketing technique.

How to place A+ Content on your book's detail page

After you fill in all the information for them, Amazon places the A+ Content on your book's Detail page.

Amazon does an excellent job of explaining how to do this. Go to your Amazon kdp account by going to kdp.Amazon.com and then log in.

Then, across the top of the page, you'll see the headings *Bookshelf, Reports, Community,* and *Marketing.* Click on the *Marketing* heading. On that page, scroll down a little, and you'll see the A+ Content box.

With A+ Content, you can add images, text, and comparison tables to your product detail page to engage readers and give more information as they consider buying your book.

You can click on the Getting Started with A+ Content, A+ Content Guidelines, or A+ Content Example links shown in the box and learn all about the benefits of adding A+ Content to your book listing and how to do it step-by-step.

To create the banners (or modules as Amazon calls them) to use as your A+ Content, you can use Canva, Photoshop, or GIMP. You can also go to Fiverr.com and have someone create the modules for you for a small fee.

You can have up to five modules in your A+ Content. You don't have to create five A+ Content modules but create at least one, and you can add more later if you want to. If you want to create your own modules, below is a link to a YouTube video showing you how to use Canva to create modules for your A+ Content.

https://www.youtube.com/watch?v=RZT4Z9EOiac

Look at some of the books in your niche that you'll be competing with and see how many of them are using the

A+ Content marketing technique. I don't think you'll find many.

By the way, the text you include in your A+ Content will not be indexed by Amazon, so don't worry about having keywords in your text. Make your text as informative and persuasive as possible to help convince readers that this book will solve their problems.

Google does index this text, so use keywords if they fit, but don't force them into the text and make it read awkwardly.

#7. Continue marketing your book

Do promotions of your book every three to six months. Make the eBook version free for two or three days again. (Use the technique described previously to do this.) Post information about your book in any newsletters or emails you send to your lists. Also, let the people on your lists know about the free days.

Let movers, shakers, and gurus in your niche know that you're available to be interviewed. If you get interviewed by them, this will put you in front of their followers, most of whom you probably wouldn't have reached otherwise.

When you're on their program, it's not your job to sell books. Your job is to provide interesting information and entertain the audience.

At the end of the interview, the interviewer will promote your book. When someone else talks about how great you and your book are, that's way better than you trying to say how good your book is. This technique sells books and keeps the buzz alive.

#8. Bonus marketing technique

Encourage your friends who are writing a review for your book to include a keyword phrase in the review. This is a new technique that not many writers are familiar with. Amazon has started ranking books based not only on what keywords and phrases are included in the title and subtitle but now they also look at the reviews to see how readers describe your book.

You don't have any control over what people say about your book in the reviews except for maybe a few close friends. When asking friends to leave a review, you can tell them that if they use one of the keywords or phrases from your title or subtitle in their review, it will help your book rank higher for that phrase.

It's not a big deal, but every little bit helps.

Miscellaneous comments about book marketing

- Send a book to your hometown newspaper. They

like to report that a "Local man (or woman) published a book." You may only sell a few books because of the reviews they do for you, but you can use anything good they say about the book in your Editorial Review section, and if they publish a review of your book, they will always say something good about it.

- Don't make your book available for preorder on Amazon. In my opinion, this technique works only if you're a well-known author and have a large following. One significant disadvantage of making your book available for preorder before it's available for purchase is that if it doesn't get a lot of preorders, Amazon will see that it has a history of very few orders. This will factor into how popular they think your book is, and they will not recommend it as aggressively.

- Set up your "Author Page" on Amazon. Your Amazon Author Page will often appear in a Google search when someone searches for your name, the name of your book, or some keywords or phrases you've optimized for. Your author page will have a strong pitch for your book, with pictures of you, an image of the book, a description of the book, and maybe even some videos. You can add those to your Author Page as you write more books. You should set up your author page before your book is even published.

- Don't spend money on advertising. It's tempting to give somebody or a company your credit card number and have them do all the marketing and make your book a #1 bestseller. Plenty of companies out there will promise to do just that. My advice is that you don't do it. Instead, spend your time and market your own book.

I've known authors who've had limited success advertising their books on Google, Amazon, Facebook Marketplace, and others. But I don't know anyone who has had significant success paying for ads to promote their nonfiction book. I assume some writers have successfully promoted their nonfiction books by using ads, but not any authors I know.

Spending money advertising your book will increase your sales, and if your only goal is to have a best-selling book, running ads will help, but if your goal is to make money with your book, I think you would be better off not advertising. I have never spent any money running ads for any of my books.

If you're determined to spend some money on advertising, go slow with a limited daily ad budget. Always test your ads by doing an A-B split where you're testing one ad against another and keep tweaking your ads.

If you have some money in your budget that you can spend on your book, spend it to help you have a better book before you spend any money advertising it. Spend your money on a better cover design or a professional proofreader, or invest in Publisher Rocket software to help you select better keywords and categories.

Writing and testing ads is a unique skill, and if you're thinking about running ads for your book, I suggest you first spend some time learning how to do it profitably. You can quickly sink a lot of money into ad campaigns when you don't know the traps and pitfalls.

Several books, videos, and courses will teach you how to run Amazon and Facebook ads. Later, if you want to try running ads, take the time to learn some skills and then start slowly. My advice is not to spend money promoting your book by running ads. I've never paid a dime for an ad to promote one of my books.

Maybe I could have sold more books if I had. But if you run an ad campaign the right way, it will take a lot of time to test, track, and modify the ads to have successful campaigns. In my opinion, it's not for the novice. I had rather spend my time writing another book.

Order an eBook and a printed book as soon as your book is available for sale on Amazon. Amazon doesn't rank your book until there is at least one sale. Pay the retail price and order the books as a regular customer. Also, I do this because I want to make sure that everything in both versions is correct.

You can order author copies for $3 or $4, but it takes a week or more to receive the printed book when you order it this way. You'll get your book in two days if you order it like a regular customer.

As soon as I'm satisfied everything about my book is like I want it to be, I'll order a dozen or two dozen books at the discounted author price to give to people to get reviews.

After the book has been on the market for a week or two, I'll start sending copies of the printed book to the movers and shakers in the industry, asking them to review the book in their newsletter, blog, on their podcast, or give me an Editorial Review I can post on my Amazon book Detail page. I remind them that they can include the name of their book, website, YouTube channel, etc., in their byline.

Remember that if your book is not selling well after you've done all of the marketing techniques described in this chapter, you can always unpublish it and update it or republish it with a different title, cover, and a lot of additional content and try again. In other words, channel most of your work towards a different niche.

Closing comments on marketing your book

So, now that you've written a good book follow the steps and techniques described in this chapter and market your book like your life depends on it. Your life as an author does depend on it.

Remember that marketing your book is an ongoing endeavor. You should always be working on getting more reviews, creating more buzz on social media, and changing some of your keywords from time to time as your book gets more popular and you can rank high for some of the more popular keywords.

One Final Point: If you're serious about learning how to market your book, check out my recent book, ***Book Marketing Magic***. It's available on Amazon. The eBook version is only $3.95. How many extra books would you have to sell to make $3.95

Here's the main takeaway from this chapter: The best way to sell more books is to do the things described in this chapter to market your book. Then, while you're continuing to market it, you should write another book.

The best way to sell more books is to write more books.

Chapter 17

Should You Publish an Audiobook Version?

"Life is short. Break the rules. Forgive quickly, kiss slowly. Love truly, laugh uncontrollably, and never regret anything that makes you smile."

~ Mark Twain

Audiobooks will expose your book to a broader audience. There are a lot of people who don't read books. Why? I don't know, but it's a fact.

48% of audiobook listeners are below 35 years old, so if your target audience is in that age range, you should seriously consider having an audiobook.

The audiobook market is growing way faster than print books or eBooks. Here are some market growth data for the past year.

Recent book sales data

- eBook sales **decreased by 5%**

- Print book sales **increased by 8%**

- Audiobook sales **increased by 32%**

You don't have to choose. Maybe you should be in all three markets. Some books don't work well as audiobooks, such as books with several pictures or links. And I wouldn't want a cookbook in an audiobook format. But for most books, you should seriously consider also publishing it as an audiobook, but only if you follow the advice in this chapter.

Whether you hire a narrator or do it yourself, you'll need to get your book ready to be read and recorded. This means you'll probably need to modify the text slightly. You can't say, "Click here," or look at the image below. I would recommend you eliminate all or almost all hyperlinks. People won't be able to remember a hyperlink, and if they're driving down the road listening to your audiobook, they won't be able to write it down.

In fiction books, there are usually a few different voices required for the different characters, so the narrator needs to be somewhat of an actor to do a good job of narrating the book. That's not the case for your nonfiction book. You can probably narrate your nonfiction book yourself.

A great place to record your audiobook is in your closet. It's probably the quietest place in your house, and the clothes will absorb and block out outside street noises and echoes.

Treat the launch of your audiobook just like you would the launch of your eBook and print book.

Audiobooks differ from printed books and eBooks in several ways. Here are some of the differences and facts about audiobooks.

- Amazon owns Audible.com.

- You don't set the price of your audiobook. Audible sets the price based on its length. Hint: you want your book to be at least three hours long, which means it should contain at least 35,000 words.

- The Audio Publishers Association says audiobook sales grew to $1.6 billion in 2021. This marks the tenth straight year of double-digit growth for the audiobook industry.

The best part about audiobooks is that there is not nearly as much competition as there is for Amazon books. For example, if you search Amazon.com for the word "RVing," Amazon says there are over 3,000 books (about 20 of those are mine), but if you search Audible.com, they say there are only 16 (and one of those is mine).

Like all of the techniques I've shown you in this book, I'll show you how you can narrate your book yourself and get your audiobook created and listed on Audible.com for zero cost.

You can also use a 50-50 royalty split and get your audiobook created by a top-notch narrator for no money out of your pocket, but I don't recommend that you do this in most cases.

Audible.com is the company Amazon owns that sells audiobooks. ACX.com is the Amazon company that produces audiobooks.

If you go to ACX.com, you can learn about the many ways you can produce your audiobook. There's a section called ACX University that teaches you all about how to create, publish, and market your audiobook.

You can spend some money and hire a narrator and get your audiobook listed faster and with a professional narrator. That's what I did.

If you go to **https://www.audible.com** and search for *"Secrets of RVing on Social Security,"* you'll find my audiobook.

Or search for *"How to Write a Nonfiction Book,"* and you'll find the audiobook version of this book.

Even if you're not a professional speaker and don't think you have a voice that people would like to listen to, there is some benefit to narrating your own book. I like to listen to nonfiction audiobooks that are narrated by the author.

By the way, if you're hiring a narrator, it's a good idea to hire one that's the same gender as you and maybe even has the same general characteristics. For example, if you're a young woman, you wouldn't want to choose an older man to narrate your book.

Three ways to create an audiobook version of your book

#1. Pay the price and hire an experienced, top-quality narrator with several reviews. (Remember that regardless of the price per finished hour a narrator is quoting, you're always free to make a lower price counteroffer; who knows, your chosen narrator may go along with your offer.)

#2. Do the narration yourself. There are a lot of advantages to narrating your own book (in addition to saving money). You'll need to watch some YouTube videos and learn the skills necessary, but you can do it.

For a fiction book, you'll probably have different characters and need other voices or inflections for the various characters. It would be helpful if your narrator were an actor, and many professional narrators are actors.

But for your nonfiction book, you should seriously consider narrating it yourself.

You're the expert, and people want to hear from you—even if you don't have a professional voice. If you've written a book to establish your credibility, become known as the expert, and build trust, maybe you should be the voice in your audience's head.

Narrating a book is hard work. It usually takes two to four hours of work to end up with one finished hour of narration. But it can save you money over hiring a professional narrator.

Just because you can narrate your book yourself doesn't mean you should do it. It depends on your skills, interests, and budget. I use freelancers to do many things I could do myself. I could design my own book covers, and I have, but I usually contract the work out to a freelancer.

Likewise, I could narrate my own audiobooks, but I decided to hire a professional narrator. I used Mike Steele to do the narration of this book. He did a great job at a reasonable price. I'll be using him to narrate my future books. He's professional and easy to work with.

Check out his website at https://www.mikes-mic.com and hear some samples of his work. There's also a "contact me" page, and he's very responsive. If you want to contact him directly, you can email him at Mike@mikes-mic.com.

#3. Hire a narrator using the 50/50 royalty split option. You'll each receive a 20% commission on each audiobook sold for the next seven years instead of getting the standard 40% royalty. I recommend you don't choose this option unless there is no possible way you can make one of the other options work for you. I would recommend this option only if you were in a situation where it's either go this route or don't produce an audiobook. Keep in mind that you can always make an audiobook later.

Here's the guaranteed way to make a profit with an audiobook. Narrate your book yourself. If you narrate your book yourself, you're guaranteed to make money because you have ZERO cost. One sale, and you've made money. You don't have to have a radio or TV announcer's voice. Just be yourself.

When someone is considering buying a fiction audiobook to be entertained, they want a pleasing voice to listen to and someone who can make the different characters come to life. But if they're considering purchasing an audiobook to solve a problem, as long as the narrator's voice is not a high-pitched, irritating voice, I don't think the voice would make much difference in their decision to buy the book.

In other words, your voice will be just fine. Don't use your voice as an excuse not to produce an audiobook.

You need a good microphone and a quiet place to do the narration. Don't try to narrate a book using a microphone built into your cell phone or a tiny Lavalier-type microphone.

Acx.com has some instructional videos, and several YouTube videos tell you how to narrate your book. The free program Audacity.com will make it easy for you to record, edit, splice, and create your audiobook. You can even use it to change the pitch of your voice.

Don't get carried away worrying about your voice. The phrase "Narrated by the author" appeals to many audiobook buyers, especially nonfiction books. They don't expect you to have the perfect voice.

Will your book sell well as an audiobook?

These guidelines help you decide if your book would likely sell well as an audiobook. Your book doesn't have to meet every benchmark to be successful, but the more you can meet, the better your chances of having a successful audiobook.

- **Will your audiobook be at least three hours long?** You'll need about 30,000 to 35,000 words in your book for it to be a three-hour-long book. Audible sets the price based on the length of the audiobook.

$3.95 - Less than 1 hour

$6.95 - 1 to 3 hours

$14.95 - 3 to 5 hours

$19.95 - 5 to 10 hours

$24.95 - Longer than 10 hours

As you can see, the sweet spot is to have an audiobook that's at least three hours long.

Note that you will receive 40% of the sales price. So, for an audiobook that's three hours long, you'll receive 40% of $14.95 or $5.98 for each audiobook sold.

- **High-priced audiobooks sell better.** Here's why: A high percentage of people buying audiobooks are on a plan where they get one or two free audiobooks a month, and they don't want to use one of their free audiobook coupons to buy a low-price audiobook.

- **Can you write another book on the same general topic?** If you have two or more audiobooks, you can bundle them. Your bundle will easily be five hours or longer. You can sell each audiobook individually and then bundle them. That way, you will have three products. Note that a book can only be included in one bundle.

- **Check your keywords.** If your keywords show between 50 and 100 results when you search for the word or phrase, that's a good indication that your audiobook will sell well. That means there is reasonable interest in the topic, but it's not overly competitive. Just like with books, you don't want to optimize for keywords that no one is searching for, but you don't want to select keywords that are so popular that you have no hope of ranking for them.

Publisher Rocket, the keyword tool described back in Chapter 3, has a unique feature that searches for keywords people are using when searching for audiobooks. You will often find that you can rank high for competitive keywords and phrases for your audiobook that you wouldn't have a prayer of ranking high for with your eBook or print book.

- **How intense is the competition for your keywords?** You would like to find keywords where the competitors have fewer than 100 reviews. You won't be able to compete if they have thousands of reviews. If you have three reviews and your competitors have 300, not many people will choose to buy your audiobook.

Equipment you'll need to record your audiobook

- **Microphone:** Yeti Blue ($80 to $120) or Audio Technica AT2020 ($100). These are both USB microphones. They plug directly into your computer.

- An XLR microphone will sound a little better, but you will need an audio interface to connect the microphone and your computer. If you use an XLR microphone, you should use balanced cables to reduce noise.

- **Audio interface:** You plug your XLR microphone into the interface and then plug the interface into your computer. Focusrite Scarlet Solo ($120) and PreSonus AudioBox USB 96 ($100) are good audio interface choices.

- **Software:** Reaper (about $60) or Audacity, which is free.

- **Storage:** To store your finished work, you can buy an external hard drive ($100) or use Dropbox or Google Drive, which cost about $100 per year.

- **Headphones:** You'll need headphones or earbuds to listen to the playbacks of your recordings.

There are several YouTube videos that will show you how to record your narration. If you're going to narrate your own audiobook, take the time to watch several of these videos.

With the right equipment and knowledge, you can create an audiobook that is better than many on the market.

Here's something to consider: After you learn how to narrate and create audiobooks, you may want to consider narrating as a new side hustle. You can sign up on ACX.

The main takeaway from this chapter: There's not nearly as much competition in the audiobook field as in printed books and eBooks. I've only recently stuck my toe in the water of the audiobook world, but it's proving profitable. I have an audiobook version of this book and one other, but I plan to create audiobooks for all of my future books. Follow the steps and information in this chapter, and you could soon be making money with your own audiobook.

Chapter 18

How to Find a Profitable Topic for Your Next Book

"Adventure is worthwhile in itself."

~ Amelia Earhart

You probably already know the topic or niche for your first book. After you write and publish your first book, you need to get busy and start writing your second book, but what topic or niche should you choose?

If you are still interested in the topic of your first book, you should write your second book on another aspect of that subject. Having several books in the same niche is a good idea because people who read your first book will likely want to read your next book on the topic.

But if you've lost interest in the topic or have decided it's not a profitable niche, this chapter will help you find a new, exciting topic.

How to choose a niche for your next book

This may surprise you, but your book doesn't have to be about a topic you know much about. But it needs to be about a topic you're extremely interested in—a topic you would like to know a lot about and would enjoy doing research to learn more about.

That's because, for just about any how-to or nonfiction book you write, you'll need to do some research—maybe even a lot of research. If nothing else, you need to know what other writers have said about the topic.

You will write a book based on your unique knowledge and opinions about the topic. Whether your knowledge came from personal experience or research doesn't matter.

Since 2008, Bill O'Reilly has written more books that ranked #1 on the *New York Times* Bestseller list than any other author, and he didn't know much about most of the topics of those books before he started doing research.

He started by doing research to find out what topics would sell. Of course, he has a lot of other things going for him, but the most important secret to his success is that he writes about topics people want to know more about.

Will your book be successful?

If the nonfiction book you're considering writing can do any of the following four things, it will significantly improve your chances of success

1. Does your book enable the reader to go from zero to hero in their world?

2. Does your book offer an unconventional solution to a problem many people face?

3. Will a lot of people who read your book say it transformed their lives?

4. Does your book provide a solution that goes against conventional wisdom?

In the case of this book, I think it could be described by #1 and #3. What do you think?

The secret to writing a successful and profitable nonfiction book

It's simple:

- **Find a topic you're interested in** and want to learn more about.

- **Make sure it's a topic that a lot of other people are interested in**. Do a little bit of book marketing research and validate your idea. Do this by going through the steps described in Chapter 3, showing how to select profitable keywords. Note: For a keyword (and topic) to be profitable for you, it must get a reasonable number of searches per month but not be so competitive that you can't rank high for the word or phrase, and it needs to be a keyword that people are spending money on. (You can't guess. You need data to confirm your hunch before you spend time and effort writing your book.)

- **Do your research** to get the information necessary to write your book. Your book doesn't have to be just your firsthand knowledge of the subject. In most cases, it should be a mixture of your knowledge, experience, and your research.

- **Then, write and publish a high-quality book**.

Only a few writers follow this technique. They spend a lot of time writing their book but almost no time going through the steps necessary to find out if there's a market for the book or whether they can successfully compete in that market. They skip all these steps, write their book, upload it to Amazon, and then wonder why nobody is buying their book.

It doesn't matter how wonderful your book is. If your book is about a topic that no one is interested in or the keywords people are searching for are so popular that you don't have a chance of ranking high for them, you're not going to sell many books.

Three other points to consider

- **Lifestyles, hobbies, crafts, and home are good general topics for new authors.** (Note that when I say "home," I'm talking about gardening, decorating, remodeling, cooking, hobbies, etc.)

- I like to select markets where the #20 book in the bestsellers list has a BSR rank of 100,000 or less.

- Look at Amazon's list of the 100 best-selling nonfiction books. (This list is updated hourly.) See if you find any topics that interest you. Looking at this list is a good place to get ideas. When you find a topic that interests you (even if you don't know much about it), consider writing a book on a different aspect of that general topic or the same topic from a different point of view.

Do the work (including the research before you write your book); find profitable keywords, publish an informative, high-quality book, market your book, and you'll make money. It's that simple.

A lot of books never get finished because the author loses interest or else they're never satisfied with their work and continually think they can tweak the book and improve it.

How much money does an author make from a book that's almost ready to be published? ZERO. Don't let that happen to you.

The main takeaway from this chapter: To find the topic for your next book, the most important thing is to find a topic you're sincerely interested in. It doesn't have to be a topic you know much about. After you find some subjects you're interested in, do your keyword research to see how profitable each of the topics you've selected would be and how competitive the crucial keywords are.

Chapter 19

Writing Books as a Side Hustle

"There's nothing to writing. All you do is sit at your typewriter and bleed."

~ Ernest Hemingway

When you're making money writing books, you can "work" anywhere.

I don't think I've ever had a good idea while sitting behind my desk. My good ideas have all come in the most unexpected places and at the most unexpected times.

How a starving writer can live high on the hog

Where wages are low, the cost of living is low. In a lot of foreign countries, the wages (if you can even get a job) are extremely low ($1.50 to $2.00 an hour).

When you can make money as a writer, you can live and "work" in beautiful, exotic places inexpensively. And when you're living in places where the cost of living is dirt-cheap, you don't have to make much money to enjoy a wonderful life.

Picture yourself "working" in the setting shown in this picture. When you're not surrounded by clutter and your mind is free to roam, I think you can see how you could be very productive here.

Picture yourself writing your next book sitting here.

I think you could be productive and turn out some excellent writing if you were in the environment shown in the above picture.

You had to learn several new skills (writing, editing, formatting, marketing, etc.) to publish your first book, but now that you've made it happen, don't stop. Immediately get started writing your next book and then your next one.

Writing is a way of life that is enjoyable, rewarding, fulfilling, profitable and gives you a level of freedom that few people ever experience.

Writing and publishing a single book could be better than having a million dollars in the bank. Let me explain.

If you had a million dollars in a savings account drawing 3% interest, you could collect $2,500 a month. (Yeah, I know you could invest the million dollars in the stock market and maybe get a 6% return, but your investment could go down too.)

I've had books that brought in $2,500 a month. That would be the same income as having a million dollars in the bank.

Some classic books have been selling well for 20 or more years, but in general, most books don't stay in the bestsellers category forever, so you'll need to keep turning out books to make sure your monthly income continues to provide you with the lifestyle you want.

Here are the expensive parts of creating and publishing a book

- Cover design

- Proofreading

- Formatting

- Narration (if you want an audiobook)

If you learn the skills to do these tasks, you can turn out books at absolutely zero cost. The one exception is that I would recommend that regardless of how good you are at proofreading, you'll still need someone else to proofread your book. Maybe you have writer friends who will do this for you at no cost. Have several people proofread your book if possible.

It's almost impossible to catch everything but put a lot of time and effort into making your book as error-free as possible.

The way I do it is that I run my manuscript through a grammar program to catch typos, grammar, and spelling errors (I use Grammarly).

Next, I use the text-to-speech feature in MS Word to have my computer read my manuscript to me. I always catch several errors when I do this.

Your mind tricks you, fills in missing words, and corrects other errors while reading text. This is especially true when you're reading your own material.

When you hear your manuscript read back to you, it's a lot easier to catch the wrong word or phrase, or to identify awkwardness or inconsistency.

Then, after correcting as many errors as possible using these two techniques, I hire a professional proofreader.

After the proofreader works miracles with my manuscript, I turn it over to several friends to read.

I don't dare let my friends read my book until I've had my proofreader work his magic. That way, my friends don't know how bad of a writer I truly am.

Remember that sometimes people suggest changes that are not necessarily right or wrong—just opinions. In other words, things can be said in different ways.

I agree with some of the suggested changes and can't entirely agree with others. I don't want to hurt anyone's feelings when I ask for their advice and then don't take it. But I always get comments and recommendations for changes I don't incorporate. After all, it's your book and your voice, so don't feel obligated to include every suggestion.

Being a digital nomad

Being a digital nomad means having zero ties to a location; in other words, you have a location-independent way to make a living.

Consider living this lifestyle for at least a short time to experience it and see what it's like. You can most likely live in places that are much less expensive than where you live now.

There's never been a better time to be a digital nomad.

The key to becoming a digital nomad is having a location-independent way to make money.

You can either work on your own projects or do gig work. You have the most freedom when working on your own projects, but the income is not guaranteed.

When you do gig work for others, you have guaranteed income, but you usually have deadlines to meet, so you're not entirely in control of your time.

Many digital nomads do some of both. Another option is to work remotely for an employer—maybe even your present employer.

When you can make money, whether you're camping in an RV next to the beach or in a coffee shop in a foreign country, you have total freedom. Right now, I'm sitting by a river in the mountains. This morning, I was in a coffee shop.

You can travel solo, with a friend, or with your family. And you can travel internationally or travel around your home country. And best of all, you can stay in any place for as long as you want.

Whether you're doing gig work or working on your own projects, you can decide to work day and night for a few days or weeks and then take time off and not do any work for a while.

It's not the purpose of this chapter to show you how to be a digital nomad but rather to open your mind to the idea of it.

The lifestyle is not for everyone. Whether you want to become a location-independent digital nomad or not is your choice. My suggestion is to try it. You might like it.

All you need is a skill and a desire to make it happen

You probably already have a marketable skill that you could take on the road, but if you don't have the skills you need, there are a lot of good books and YouTube videos that will teach you what you need to know. Books and YouTube videos are what I use when I want to learn a new skill.

Another option is that you can take online courses through Skillshare.com or Udemy.com. The classes are not expensive.

My primary source of income is writing, and I'm constantly watching videos and reading articles about ways to improve my writing and better market my books.

I can do my writing from anywhere, but I'm more productive in remote, out-of-the-way places. Keep in mind that your mindset is more important than your skill set when it comes to being a successful digital nomad.

Earn your first digital nomad dollar in the next 90 days.

Don't just think about it. Set a goal to pick a project or gig and make some money as a digital nomad in the next 90 days. Learn a skill if you need to. It's not important how much you earn. It's just important that you make your first digital nomad dollar within 90 days.

If you choose to work on your own project, such as writing a book, starting a YouTube channel, designing a course, or starting a subscription website, these will take longer, but you can still earn money within a few months.

Maybe your digital nomad income could cover all of your Christmas shopping—if not this year, maybe next year for sure. Just a thought.

Consider using Fiverr.com to get a gig. Whether you want to do proofreading, graphic design, book formatting, book cover design, logo design, ghostwriting, or any one of hundreds of other gigs, you can find location-independent work on Fiverr.com.

Not only can you find work on Fiverr.com or UpWork.com, but you can also have work done for you to help speed your projects along. I have a guy I found on Fiverr who lives in Bulgaria (Ken, who goes by **MrProofreader**), and he does a great job of proofreading my books. By the way, he's from Texas, but since he is working as a digital nomad, he's free to live anywhere in the world. He used to live in Croatia.

One good thing about the digital nomad lifestyle is that your decisions don't have to be permanent. When you're a digital nomad, you can change almost anything about your lifestyle at the drop of a hat.

One last point: Don't spend your time creating low-content and no-content books. It's a fad, and even though some people have made a lot of money doing it, my recommendation is to write a real book. By low-content and no-content books, I'm talking about logbooks, journals, etc.

Summary

With the combination of writing books plus doing some freelance work using your newly acquired skills of formatting, cover design, narration, and maybe even proofreading, you really can be a badass, location-independent digital nomad. You may find that writing books, plus your other newly acquired skills, can be more than a side hustle for you. It could allow you to live a whole new lifestyle.

You have to decide to do it, do some research, learn some skills if necessary, and then make it happen. As I've said before, it's not the skill set but the mindset that will determine whether this lifestyle will work for you.

The main takeaway from this chapter: When you can make money writing books, you'll have the ultimate side hustle. You can go anywhere, live anywhere, and you'll be free to live in a different place at the drop of a hat. Best of all, where you live will be your choice because you'll have a location-independent source of income. You'll be free to live part-time in some beautiful, exotic places for a fraction of what you're spending to live now. You can make all of this happen with zero risk if you write a book or two and get money coming in before you start living your location-independent lifestyle.

Chapter 20

Closing Thoughts

"Not all storms come to disrupt your life. Some come to clear your path."

~ Paulo Coelho (Best-selling novelist)

I don't think Paulo's comment would apply if you lived on a sailboat, but that's a subject for another day. Let's get back to writing your book.

Make sure you have a quality book. That includes the cover, the title, the subtitle, and the grammar. Make sure all the links work, you don't have typos, and the format looks professional.

You will never have a successful book if the quality is not there.

Spend time and effort to produce a quality book. You don't want to put your name on a crappy book.

I don't know how many times I've seen a book review that said, "The author should have hired a professional proofreader." I've also seen comments like, "There were so many grammar errors and typos that I stopped reading the book."

Reviews like this will kill your book sales. You can go back and fix the problems, but the review will be there forever.

A lesson I learned the hard way

As I mentioned before, one time, I published a book with several links, and I didn't format all of the links correctly in the eBook version. Some of them were not clickable. Someone posted a review and said that the links didn't work. Sales dropped off almost immediately.

I quickly corrected the problem and made the links clickable, and then I posted a reply to the comment saying that the links were now clickable, but almost nobody reads answers to review comments. The book never recovered, and that book never sold well. That was years ago, and that review is still there.

What's that old saying about never getting a second chance to make a first impression?

One other point. Include what's called a "Lead Magnet" in your book. A lead magnet is something that will enable you to add your customers' names and email addresses to your list. The easy way to do this is to give the reader something free in exchange for their name and email address.

You don't phrase it that way. You say, "I would like to send you a free (whatever). Click on this link (or go to this website) and leave me your first name and email address, and I'll send it to you immediately."

What you'll be sending should be something of high perceived value. It should be something related to the topic of your book, such as a checklist, a template, a special report, or anything of high perceived value that you can send by email.

I made a huge mistake by not including a lead magnet in my last 20+ books. Imagine the size of my mailing list if I had collected email addresses and names all these years.

I did include a lead magnet in this book. Here it is

Go to https://aLaptopLife.com and leave me your first name and email address, and I'll send you my free Special Report, *Advanced Book Marketing Techniques.* I'll also add you to the list to receive my **Book Marketing Tip of the Week**. You can cancel at any time.

Having a mailing list of your customers is extremely valuable. Promoting your future books is one of the best things you can do with it.

Will your first book be a smashing success?

Your first book has a good chance of being super successful because you will put your heart and soul into it.

Royalties from my first book have been over $70,000, and it's still selling well. Royalties from my second book have been over $50,000 so far.

Would having a few books like this change your life?

Follow the advice and techniques described in this book, write and publish a quality book on a topic many people are interested in, and then do two more things.

Market your book and get busy writing your next book. You can do both at the same time.

The secret to being a successful author is written on your shampoo bottle—lather, rinse, and repeat. In other words, write, publish, and repeat.

Here are a few authors who have made over a million dollars from their first book. You can do it too

- John Locke's first book, *Lethal People*, earned him over a million dollars in royalties within the first six months after it was self-published.

- Emma Cline published her first book, *The Girls*, in

2016 and was paid $2 million in advance before the book was even completed. Imagine being paid $2 million in advance when you have never published a book in your life.

- Amanda Hocking wanted to attend an event in Chicago. She was willing to drive the eight hours from her apartment in Minnesota to get there, but she didn't have the money for gas or a hotel when she got there. Amanda needed to raise $300 to attend the event and had six months to raise the money. She had never sold a book in her life, but she decided to try selling her book on Amazon. (Umpteen agents had turned down her book.) She made over $20,000 during those six months, and within the next 18 months, she made over $2.5 million.

I could fill this book with stories about successful authors selling their first books on Amazon. There's no reason why your first book can't be a smashing success.

I would love to include your success story in the next version of this book.

You can be a successful writer.

It doesn't matter if you don't think you can write. Here's all you have to do to be a successful writer.

- Find a topic you're genuinely interested in (and

one that a lot of other people are interested in.)

- Do the research to get the information you need.

- Write like you were talking to a friend.

- Hire a proofreader to correct your grammar and typos.

- Publish your book and market the heck out of it.

That's all it takes, and you can do it.

When you publish your book, let me know at **jminchey@gmail.com** when it's 99¢, and I will buy a copy, read it, and leave you a review.

I'm looking forward to reading your book.

Note: Send me a PDF copy before your book is published, and I'll send you an **Editorial Review** that you can include on your Detail page.

Two New Books: I have recently published two new books that you might find helpful.

- **Book Marketing Magic:** How to Market A Nonfiction Book

- **Book Editing Guide:** How To Edit Your First Book

Chapter 21

Did You Like This Book?

If you liked this book, I need your help.

I would love it if you would take a minute and leave a review on Amazon. (You can do it in less than a minute.)

I read and appreciate every review.

Writing a review is not like writing a high school book report. All you need to do is write a sentence or two saying that you liked the book.

If you liked anything in particular (such as the techniques, the writing style, the details, etc.), you could point that out, but if nothing comes to mind, don't worry about it. The important thing is to get a review submitted. What it says is not so important.

Thank you,

Jerry Minchey

P.S. Take a look at the right side of my website, **LifeRV.com**and you can see a list of my other books. Click on any of them, and it will take you to the book on Amazon.

Made in the USA
Middletown, DE
17 July 2024

57421576R00126